stephanie pearl-mcphee

New York Times best-selling author

The Amazing Thing

About the Way It Goes

Stories of Tidiness, Self-Esteem,
and Other Things I Gave Up On

Andrews McMeel
Publishing®

Kansas City • Sydney • London

Also by Stephanie Pearl-McPhee

Yarn Harlot

Free-Range Knitter

All Wound Up

Andrews McMeel Publishing, LLC
an Andrews McMeel Universal company
1130 Walnut Street, Kansas City, Missouri 64106
www.andrewsmcmeel.com

www.yarnharlot.ca

14 15 16 17 18   RR2   10 9 8 7 6 5 4 3

ISBN: 978-1-4494-3708-4

Library of Congress Control Number: 2013916581

ATTENTION: SCHOOLS AND BUSINESSES

Andrews McMeel books are available at quantity discounts with bulk purchase for educational, business, or sales promotional use. For information, please e-mail the Andrews McMeel Publishing Special Sales Department: specialsales@amuniversal.com.

Contents

Another for my book-loving uncle Tupper,
with profound regret that what he really wanted me
to write couldn't be written until after he had to go.
Neither of us have ever had great timing.

Acknowledgements

As with everything good I have ever made, this book would be a twisted train wreck if I were in it alone.

First, my thanks to the good folks at Andrews McMeel Publishing, who had faith where I didn't. Thanks to my old editor, Lane Butler, who saw this book through its pregnancy, and my new editor, Christine Schillig, who somehow jumped on a running horse, figured out how it worked, and then brought it home.

Thanks to my agent, Linda Roghaar, who always knows what do to, even though I am probably rather crazy.

To my friends, who have been read to, cried at, and endured endless discussions about this book—long after any other people would have admitted they were tired of it and begged me to stop.

Last, but never least, to my family. This book was born during a remarkable year for us, and without their help, support, and leeway, there would be no book at all.

In particular, my long-suffering husband Joe remains a man of incredible kindness, intelligence, sensitivity, and good humor, even when he's trashing the kitchen.

Thirteen

As I lay bleeding in the dirt, I was thinking about the mistakes I had made in my life that had brought me to this moment. I was tangled in my bike and couldn't get up, but I wasn't bleeding a lot, so there was no reason to rush. I've tried to be a mostly good person, and other than that mean thing I did to Suzanne T. in grade eight, I don't think I really belonged where I was. I admit, I had made a decision that was pretty inexplicable, considering that the sport I do best is knit. I had been inspired by someone to get involved with a long-distance charity bike ride to Montréal, all the way from Toronto. About four hundred cyclists were to ride together for six days, covering 660 kilometers (410 miles), and as I lay there, I tried to remember who I had thought I was when I signed up. I've got a soft spot for epic adventure, but cycling? What had made me think I was that kind of person?

Peer pressure is usually at the top of my list of reasons for doing such things, and a lot of people I knew had done this ride and lived. My best friend, Ken, had done it, but he hadn't so much inspired me as impressed me, since he is almost terrifyingly fit and competent and he has an excellent sense of proprioception, which is to say that he almost always knows where his body is in time and space, and he seldom walks into things. There are a thousand things that Ken can do that I am never going to be able to manage; miracles like walking through the house without smashing his hip on a table or falling up the stairs. Two of my three daughters had already done it, and the youngest was signed up, but as impressed with them as I was, their commitment wasn't what set me on the path either. I was proud of them, but they were young and perfect and teenagers, and they'd never be any stronger or more lovely than they were when they did that ride, and I know that I'm past the days when I could just blast through anything. I didn't class myself with them for a moment. My sister, though, she had done the ride and lived to tell the tale, and that's what got me. Erin's not sporty. Erin doesn't jog. Erin's only five years younger than me and not really fitter than me. The only functional difference between Erin and me is that she accessorizes, but to my way of thinking that likely wasn't what made it possible for her to pack up one summer and ride her bike for six straight days like it was a job.

That, I thought as I moved my head off a rock, might not be totally true, or it might be, or who the hell knew, because if training for this ride had revealed anything to me it was that somewhere, somehow, there was some other tiny little difference between Erin and me, some magical string of genes that was on her code and not mine—something that may be related to how her hair always looks cute and mine doesn't. Whatever it was that made Erin want to find a matching scarf for an outfit, apparently that gene sits on her DNA right next to whatever it is that keeps a human being from falling off a bike, because there I was, off my bike, lying in the dirt, bleeding, and it wasn't the first time. It was the thirteenth. I already had so many cuts, bruises, and abrasions that I didn't look so much like I'd taken up riding a road bike but rather like I had been beaten with one. I spat out a bug that had crawled in the side of my mouth and resolved to lie there a little longer.

I've been riding a bike since I was five, and, aside from this phase, there have been little to no difficulties. There was the year that I rode into a ditch on Prince Edward Island, but it was dark, and I didn't lose control of the bike or my faculties. I just lost track of where the road was for a minute and cycled straight into the abyss. It made sense, it was really the only accident I'd had in years and years, and the worst part about it wasn't even falling off my bike. It was that my family didn't really see that I'd dropped off the radar and left me there, lying amongst the lupines in the dark. Even as a kid—a remarkably klutzy and bruised kid—I'd always managed my bike okay, and the worst bike accident I could call to mind was one that Erin had. One summer day, when she was about ten years old, she'd learned to swoop side to side on her bike, like some great wheeled bird, and I'd gotten her to show my friends what she could do when one big swoop (empowered by ten-year-old bravado) went a little wide and Erin went straight over the handlebars. She just about knocked her teeth out, and there was an emergency room visit and blood and gore, as well as a little perpetual guilt that I'd been the one encouraging her to try it, but the important thing to think about now is that I was unequivocally not the one who had that bad accident. Erin did, and that was on a bike and, as far as I could think, that meant that she was no more coordinated than I was (except with accessories), and that emboldened me. If she could do it, so could I.

The training rides for the Friends for Life Bike Rally start a few months in advance. I showed up for the first one and noticed a few things straightaway. First, out of the few hundred riders, I was the only one on a big, clunky bike. Second, I was slower than almost all of them. I also noticed that I had more body hair than anyone there, even though the majority of them were men, but, as much as they might like to believe so, I didn't think that was what made them faster. I was pretty sure it was the bikes, so the next day I went to the bike shop and got a road bike. It was turquoise (like my big, clunky bike, which meant that now I had the start of a fleet), and the gal at the shop assured me that turquoise was the fastest color. (Apparently red only looks the fastest. It's an illusion, I was assured. At the time, I believed her, but now I wonder what she'd have said if I had tried to buy a yellow one.) Since it was a road bike, it had clipless pedals, and that meant I had to clip in.

Clipless pedals are the wildest thing. First of all, their name is inappropriate, considering what they do. You wear special shoes that have little cleats on the bottom that attach to the pedals. You clip in by attaching your feet to the bike, then swing your heel out to unclip and free your feet when you want to stop. When I heard about them, I thought they were nothing short of insane. Attaching your feet to the pedals to make it easier to ride seemed savvy, I grant you that, but there was another side to the efficiency game, which is that you and the bike are now a unit. Once you're joined, it's impossible to put your foot down on the ground without first unclipping, and that seemed like a risky layer of complexity. While I was moving I could pull up and push down on the pedals, which does let you use energy more efficiently, but how efficient was a broken leg going to be?

The first time I tried riding the road bike, I didn't go anywhere. I put on those crazy shoes and took my bike in the house and set it up in the hall, where I could hold on to two walls while I practiced. Clip, unclip, clip, unclip, clip, unclip. I thought that if I did it enough maybe I would stand a chance. It went pretty well. I felt braver, so I took my bike to the back gate and did the same thing, holding on to the gate frame as I kept trying. Clip, unclip, clip, unclip, clip, unclip. It seemed okay, and I remembered that the guy who sold me the things had said that it was easy to learn, and it would become second nature.

The next morning, I boldly embarked and fell down about nine seconds later at the bottom of my driveway. I was trying to turn, and the rear wheel skidded on gravel, and ordinarily I would put my foot down, but there wasn't time to remember the unclipping part, and there I was, splayed out on the asphalt. I went down so hard I think I heard my cat gasp.

There's something about grown-up falling. When you're little, it's no big deal. Little kids do it all the time. They scrape their knee, get a kiss on the boo-boo, and five minutes later they're back up at whatever threw them on the ground. By the time you're in your forties, though, you start worrying about falling. It's farther to the ground; it takes more to get up; seeing your blood is a little scarier than it should be. Falling can make you paranoid and weird when you're an adult, as if it could happen again at any moment, even though you're not doing anything that should hurt you. You're slower and more cautious in the world for a little while after a fall, as if there's mental caution-tape up around the whole joint. That fall was like that for me. I was bloodied and sore and bruised, but the worst part was that it opened a door to falling that I hadn't really worried about before, and I worried plenty after. The next day, I fell into a curb at the corner as I tried to obey a stop sign. I couldn't get my foot out of the clip and, inexplicably, stayed committed to stopping.

As the bike came to a standstill, over I went. I think that was the day my neighbor started watching.

The weeks went on and, much to my shame, I kept falling. One spectacular day, I crossed the street to stop next to another cyclist, successfully unclipped my right foot to set it down on the ground, and then somehow tipped my bike left and rolled into the street in front of oncoming traffic with my bike on top of my body, still attached. I flopped there in the street, with cars coming to a screeching halt, and I was panicking, thrashing in a terrible impression of an urban mermaid, the bike fused where my tail would be. The other cyclist leapt off his bike, lifted mine up, and helped me extricate myself. Blood trickled down my leg and arm, and he gave me a sympathetic look. "New clips?" he asked and smiled knowingly. I was reassured by this and nodded gravely. "It happens," he said. "You're not a real cyclist until you've fallen in your clips once."

I rode to my mum's house then, because her place was closer than mine, and tried to remember that pain is just weakness leaving the body. (I don't really believe that, but I heard an athlete say it once, and I was trying to get on board.) The other rider had said you're not a real cyclist until you've fallen over trying to unclip, but he said "once." What are you if you've fallen twelve times? I can't see how it would really be a world of increasing return. I mean, if I fall over once I'm a real cyclist, but can every fall after that make me more of one? As my mum handed me gauze and antiseptic, and I noted that I'd scraped an old scrape and reopened it, my mother looked over my broken and battered body and said what I'd been thinking. "Maybe, darling," she said gently as she helped me blot blood off of my elbow, "maybe you're not a natural."

I would have been angry, but I was starting to be afraid she was right. I showed up for the next training ride anyway and had a catastrophic fall. I was riding uphill when it happened, and, as further proof that I was struggling with the sport, it happened when I had decided to quit riding uphill. The hill was too steep, it was so hot outside that it was like trying to ride up the surface of Mercury, and my thighs were screaming in agony and forming a political group to lobby my brain for secession. I could feel a vein on my forehead that I thought might explode if I didn't quit riding for a minute or maybe forever, and I remembered that this was a choice and that there was no law that said I had to ride up that hill all in one go, and I decided to stop. I even remembered how to stop.

The thing is that I was under so much duress that I forgot about gravity. I stopped pedaling, the bike came to an instant halt, and I realized there was going to be no opportunity to unclip. I panicked. I panicked so thoroughly and completely that it is a miracle of the highest order that I remembered to try to keep pedaling until I could unclip, but it was a hill, and it was too late, and I just wasn't strong enough to overcome the forces against me. As I strained, the planet pulled and the bike went down, and I didn't just fall off, I fell backward down the hill with the bike attached to me. The rest was pretty fast, and I don't want to describe it—for my sake, not yours. I can tell you that by the time I extricated myself from my bike I had a bunch of scrapes and cuts and bruises, but worst of all, the first part of my body to connect with the road had been my arse, and the bruise that developed on the left side of it was the size of a dinner plate and so swollen that for a week when I sat in chairs I had a list to the left. I texted pictures of it to my friends.

That was the worst accident I'd had and the scariest. The fact that I was falling down a hill meant that I fell for a split second longer than I'd been expecting to. For that fraction of an instant, it seemed I'd fall forever, and it had scared me silly. Worse, I'd fallen in front of a few people I felt like I had to be brave for, so I managed somehow to get back up and back on, and I didn't let the tears come until I was riding and nobody could see me. That was my twelfth fall. I'd heard so much about how a few tumbles were pretty normal, but this? The worst part was that I had had twelve while being careful. Really careful. As a matter of fact, I had fallen off my bike twelve times in about eight weeks while doing everything possible to avoid it. I was so freaked by then that I unclipped my foot if I saw a squirrel. I no longer felt like my learning curve could possibly be normal. I would expect someone to fall off a lot in the beginning, and then to fall less and less frequently until it became rare. Me, I hadn't even started to taper off yet. I was still falling at least once a week with no end in sight. I wondered, spiritually speaking, how much longer I could take it.

I did the math. What if I was never going to improve? For every 150 kilometers (93 miles) of training, I had fallen down at least once. The length of the rally meant that, at this rate, over the course of the six-day ride I could expect to become one with the earth against my will at least four times. The idea struck terrible and complete fear into my heart. Up until that day, almost all of my incidents had been witnessed by strangers. The idea of falling down in front of people I couldn't just ride away from, people I would be riding with for days and days, was humiliating. Two words rippled through me: "Riding with." I was going to be riding with people. Suddenly I could think of a thousand ways that the falling could be worse. I imagined falling as all four hundred of us were riding along and turning myself into a human speed bump, or falling and beginning a terrible domino-style event, my fellow riders lying in a tangled mass of broken bodies and bikes. I imagined falling in front of people I liked, people who thought I was a cyclist with a right to be there, and I imagined the organizers sitting around in a meeting talking about what was going to be done about me, drawing straws to see who was going to go talk to me about how my supernatural lack of ability was endangering everyone. They would all be at a secret night meeting, saying things like, "Her heart is in the right place" and "I've never seen anything like it. Why doesn't she quit?" Then they'd all flinch, remembering the part where several people had run over my face.

Why wasn't I quitting? It was an excellent question. I'd started this whole thing only to live up to a challenge. Wasn't it okay to quit? I'm good at lots of other things, and if, as it appeared to be true, I wasn't a natural, when was the point at which a smart woman would lie in the dirt and say, "No more"? Was I there? What sort of a woman just kept getting back up? When did persistence become stupidity? When was it time to say that this was simply something I wasn't going to be good at, like laundry, making pie, or keeping houseplants alive?

All of this is what I was thinking about while I lay in the dirt. I'd been riding along, thinking about nothing except for unclipping, and watching for chances to unclip, and being prepared to unclip at all times. (As you can imagine, this made for a fairly intense ride, emotionally speaking.) I'd been getting ready to cross a bridge, and I saw an oncoming cyclist. I had decided to cycle past him, then realized the path was narrower than I thought and at the last minute had figured out I needed to stop. Something backfired, I couldn't get my foot free, and there was no room to keep going, no place to turn off. As the other cyclist headed for me, I slowly came to a stop and then fell helplessly over, scraping the better part of myself along the metal guardrail to the ground before landing in the dirt.

The look on the face of the rider approaching was priceless, if you enjoy humiliation. As I fell, he registered confusion, then horror. This guy didn't know my feet were stuck to my bike. To him, it must have looked like I had simply decided to stop pedaling and then fell over, making absolutely no attempt to save myself in any way. I went down hard and stayed there. I knew that I was still attached to the bike, and while I was getting good at that mermaid move, it was inelegant, and I didn't want to share the moment. The cyclist stopped just short of where I lay unmoving on the ground and looked at me incredulously. I blinked to show him I wasn't dead, but I didn't move. "Oh my God!" he said, and started to get off his bike. "You fell off! Are you okay?"

I'd rather not discuss the things I wanted to say, the way I wanted to call him Captain Obvious, the way I wanted to scream, "Do I look okay to you?!" But mostly I just wanted him to go away. I was suddenly exhausted by the humiliation, and the way this kept happening, and the way I was clearly not a natural. He didn't need to know that this was my thirteenth fall. He didn't need to help me, and I didn't want help. I just wanted to lie there alone and think over all my life choices while hoping that this time my bike was broken beyond repair. "I'm fine," I said, but I still didn't try to get up.

"Can you move?" he asked, clearly concerned about spinal injuries. He took out his phone.

"I'm fine," I answered, and realized that I was close to tears. "Please, just leave me here." Our eyes met for a minute, and I don't know what he saw there, but he put his phone back in his pocket, said he was sorry, and rode away.

Meeting another cyclist on that trail was rare, so I was able to lie there in privacy after that. I thought about falling down thirteen times, and something in me snapped. I made a decision. There is a number of times a woman can fall off her bike and lie in the dirt, and I suspect that number is deeply personal. For me, it turned out to be thirteen. I vowed, lying there with bugs crawling on me and my head in the ferns, that this was my personal Waterloo. Thirteen was my number, and if I fell again, I was quitting. If I fell again, I was going to sell the bike, give my apologies to the rally organizers, and tell them they could keep the money I'd raised, but that I couldn't do it. I would tell them that I had thought I was the kind of person who could do it, but that I wasn't, and I would go back to knitting, which had only ever caused me minor injuries and never landed me in the road with a car aimed at my head. I'd go back to my clunky bike and using it to fetch beer, wine, and roses. I had thought that I could undertake an epic, and I had thought I was another kind of person, but my number was thirteen.

I struggled up then and dusted myself off, firm in my commitment. I got on my bike and rode away, and something changed. I don't know what. I don't know if it was the decision, or if I just needed to know that there could only be one more fall, or if maybe the fates looked down and saw that the jig was up on this particular test, or maybe I'd finally learned everything a road bike had to teach me, but after that, things changed. I did the rest of the training rides, and I showed up on the appointed day and I rode my bike to Montréal, and when I crossed the finish line, I did it upright and without a scratch on me. What's more, I've kept cycling, and I've made the trip to Montréal again, and sometimes now I talk to beginners. When they show up with scabs and scrapes, I hear people tell them that everyone falls down once, and then I can't help myself. I take them aside, and I say, "Or thirteen. You might not be a natural. It might be thirteen."

I wonder what else in my life I would have missed out on if I only did the things that were natural for me, but mostly I wonder, as I ride along, with the wind in my helmet and the sun on my strong and scarred legs, if maybe there really is a fine line between persistence and stupidity, and maybe I stopped just short of it.

I like riding now, and it hasn't gotten easy, but I have never fallen again. You should know, though, that I mean it when I say that I'm still prepared to quit. You have to draw a line, and mine is thirteen.

Marks Left on You

We all understand and accept that we're shaped by the things that happen to us. There are people who come through wars and are forever changed. There are people who have terrible traumas of other types—disasters, catastrophes, crime, famine, or even accidents of the human heart—that don't seem as bad as a war but scar people up on the inside just the same. I know several people who are struck dumb with terror if a plane doesn't do quite what they're expecting, but I also have a friend who, twenty-five years after leaving a guy who used to clear out her bank account every five minutes of their relationship (and then buy her flowers with her own money as an apology), still changes her bank password every few months, just to be sure that he can't ever do it again. She hasn't seen the guy in a quarter century, but it was so horrible that she can't change her behavior. Experiences leave marks on people, and we might not be able to see them, but they are there, guiding our actions and decisions and making you do things like close the curtains in the bathroom every day for the rest of your life because of the one day that creepy guy your husband hired to fix the rain gutter was looking in. (He was later arrested for building a cage in his basement where he was going to keep his ex-wife's best friend right after he kidnapped her, so I was bang on the money there.)

We are, for better or worse, the sum of our experiences. There are people who don't care for apples because they were raised on an apple farm and they've hit their lifetime exposure limit for apples. I bet there are also people who love apples because they were raised on an apple farm and it was the happiest time of their life. Just the scent of applesauce could maybe transport them and lift their mood. My own mother was trained out of left-handedness in school. I can't imagine what it took to change it, but that isn't the point. The point is that she had an experience made up of twenty-seven thousand corrections that have made her who she is—someone who is left-handed but uses a pen with her right hand. There are seventy-five-year-old men who were in the military for five years and have been out for fifty, but they're still lining up their shoes and putting sharp corners on the blankets on the bed because that sort of discipline is hard to break. Personally, I'm afraid of spiders, and I can outline for you, after a bottle of wine and the establishment of some intimacy between us, exactly what the reason for that is. There was one night, and the experience will not only never let me relax around them but also won't let me understand why you can.

Understanding all this, I was so shocked to see surprise in the eyes of my friends when I told them that, more than anything else, parenting gave me most of my crazy reflexes, phobias, and wild skills, as surely as a jaunt as a Navy SEAL would have. I know I am not alone, so I don't know why they didn't want to admit it. Perhaps because we associate scars with trauma, and there isn't a mother alive who wants to say that her children were really that traumatic or perhaps admit that her children trained her, rather than the other way around, but is it really that surprising once you think a little about the training methods that human babies and children employ? Their tactics are so good, so sound, that all over the world, military forces use the same strategies for both indoctrination and torture. Sleep deprivation, noise, enforcement of consequences if you don't toe the line—just to help you understand their power. Did you know that the sound a siren makes is modeled on a human infant's cry because adults find it so irritating that they're almost helpless to ignore it? Think that over. Babies and children do the impossible. They enslave us, take our money, hurt our feelings, repeatedly frighten us near to death, ruin our possessions, erase our free time and the goals we had for ourselves, and very nearly push every parent to the limit of human existence, and yet somehow leave us completely in love, willing to die for them, convinced no person could be cuter. Cults are less compelling, and we have deprogramming experts who have to tie you up in a hotel room for three weeks to get you out of one of those.

The sort of life this makes parents lead changes them in a way that can't be undone. I know that it's left its mark on me. I had three babies in a row, all arriving within about six years. There's pretty much no way out of the consequences of that— the largest of which was not only the unbelievable way that I had some other person's bodily fluid on my clothing just about every day for many years, but also that I didn't have a single solid night's sleep in more than a decade. For at least ten straight years, every night for more than three thousand nights, at some point some person, and occasionally more than one, would wake me up at a nonspecific time and ask me to do something. This varied. Usually I just had to feed someone (that was the easiest, and I was always grateful that breastfeeding meant that I didn't have to stand up), but sometimes I was jolted from a deep sleep and needed to clean up things (usually human waste), and other times I had to come up with a complex emotional comfort system for a frightened human being who had somehow come to believe that their home had monsters in it.

This training changed me. Before I had kids, if you woke me in the night, I was bleary, disoriented, and resentful. Now, I can leap out of bed, snap to a fully alert state in a heartbeat, snatch up a sick child, and nurse and rock them back to sleep while stripping their wet bed, locating a lost stuffed hippo, and throwing in a load of laundry without a slip of trouble, and the odds are decent that I won't be resentful at all. I probably won't even remember it in the morning. I could start a black-ops team that did only night raids and it wouldn't bother me a bit, and, you know, I'd make everyone on my team someone who breastfed for a few years. There's nobody like someone who can attach a tiny person with teeth and no sense of empathy to their nipples nine times a night for a year or three and think nothing of it. You think your sniper fire is going to rattle her?

If I ever heard on the news that the alien invasion I've always worried about had finally started to happen, I tell you who I would pick up on my way to a remote safe house. Women and men who have been on a field trip to a major museum with a class of eleven-year-olds. Those people have nerves of steel and, I tell you, eyes in the backs of their heads. You don't know what unflappable is until you've seen one person responsible for not losing twelve kids while keeping them from breaking expensive things. It's like watching a damn ninja. The next time the government needs to rescue a few diplomats from a consulate, let me know. I can save them so much money on training military troops, because yesterday I saw Louise Redmond from down the street pull off her daughter's seventh birthday party nine hours after her husband came down with the stomach flu and barfed his way into uselessness, and then halfway through the party sixteen extra kids showed up, including that boy from down the street who could die if he eats a dairy product. It turns out that her daughter had invited every single stinking kid from her class and the little terrorist hadn't said a word of warning to her own mother. Do you have any idea what that woman has been through? Do you know what happens when there's not enough cake to go around at a birthday party like that? The woman is made of steel. I've never seen anything like it. Later that night, we had a glass of wine on the front porch while I got the gum out of her hair, and I asked her how she did it. She shot me a look I've only seen on prisoners of war and mumbled, "Never surrender."

I have no idea why spy agencies aren't recruiting all of their operatives at a high school parent/teacher night. I can tell if a teenager is lying in less than two seconds, and I don't need any equipment to do it. Mark, the guy around the corner? He's got five sons between fifteen and twenty-two, and he told me that he can search any room for drugs or contraband in under three minutes and you'll never know he was there. Joe asked him what he did if the door was locked, and he just shrugged. Kate Armstrong's sweet daughter fell pregnant at fifteen, and I know for a fact that Kate's heart was broken, and yet I never saw that woman cry. She was a rock, and she was there for her kid no matter what, and I wouldn't have double-dog dared anyone to say a word against her daughter. If she was disappointed, angry, or hurt, that was between her and her pillow at night. If you need a spy who won't reveal anything, no matter how much they are tortured? Screw James Bond, you need Kate. She has more practice.

Loving a kid, like everything else that's not necessarily traumatic but big and encompassing, changes you. It leaves marks on you. It creates skills and reflexes, and things are done to you that can never be undone. I know this because I see what happens in the bank. If you're in the bank and somewhere in the queue there is a baby, when that baby starts to cry, you will be able to spot every parent in the place. One by one, like soldiers answering a call to arms, or like dogs helpless to ignore a whistle no other species can hear, every parent in the place starts to sway. If the crying continues, the attempts get more earnest. Bobbing, maybe doing a little bounce, every mum and dad in that bank, no matter how old their kids are, all of a sudden each of them is executing a public version of their own child's baby dance, trying desperately to rock someone else's baby to sleep— a baby they aren't even holding.

I wonder about that. I know it's human nature to answer a child's call, and most people are instinctively good parents, and there's nothing like years of having to respond to a cry to leave you helpless to ignore it, but I don't think it's just that we've got leftover reflexes. Human beings don't like to waste energy, and bouncing and swaying to rock a baby who's not yours or even in your arms is wasteful, so, other than the boot camp our kids sent us to, why do it? Why have the training last for your whole life? I used to think it was just a mark of our mutual trauma, but now I think it's more. I think it's a way of helping each other. Of showing another parent what to do, so that if there's a new parent in the bank, traumatized and frightened, not quite sure what to do with this squalling bundle of humanity, all they have to do is look up, and there we are. Forty people who have been there, all silently telegraphing instructions and suggestions as we sway, bob, and rock in the line.

Metal Tornado

I love horrible disaster movies. Despite being an almost tragically practical realist, one of my favorite ways to relax if things in my life get crappy is to sit down with my knitting and watch the ruination of the earth. It's a family joke. One of the kids will see a movie title like *Snowmageddon* and know that I would immediately rearrange my schedule to fit it in. I don't know what I like about them exactly. Maybe it's the way that it makes all my problems seem so trifling when I'm watching freak hailstones the size of cars ruin Chicago, or maybe it's the way that I just can't believe the creativity that goes into coming up with them or even what effects they can manage, considering that the budget was probably borrowed from someone's mum, but I am absolutely smitten. If I had to choose, I would say my absolute favorites are the ones with comets or meteors about to strike the earth and wipe out mankind as we know it. The plot's always about the same. An undervalued minor player in the astronomy field, sometimes even a teenager with a $35 telescope, spots a meteor headed for our planet that everyone else has missed. They must struggle to convince NASA of the peril and then usually end up vindicated in a meeting with the president of the United States, and together with a bumbling and occasionally drunken ex-pilot or soldier, they come up with a plan to save the world or at least the teenager's girlfriend.

Considering my nature, the impressive thing about these movies is that they are able to suspend the part of me that can't get past things that make no sense. Nothing makes me crazier faster than something that can't possibly be true. I'm the person who fact checks spam e-mails that say that using a cell phone at a gas station can blow everyone up, and then writes a reply notifying the sender that it's an urban legend. I never fall for chain letters. I would never consider, even for one moment, entertaining the possibility that a real complete stranger in Dubai needs my help setting up a bank account because they're desperate to give me a million dollars before they die of cancer. I instinctively know that drinking hydrogen peroxide doesn't cure cancer, because I know two things would be true if it did. There would be a lot less cancer, and hydrogen peroxide wouldn't be a dollar a bottle.

I enjoy accuracy. Yay, verily, I am normally compelled to correct inaccuracies, even when it does me no social favors. I am the lady who will lean over, after you've told your kid that gum stays in their tummy for seven years if they swallow it, and whisper, "No. It doesn't." Similarly, I can't let you say that shaving any part of your body will make the hair grow back thicker, because I know how hair follicles work, and I can't forget that just because you want me to. Similarly, you can't actually get pregnant from swimming, no matter what is in the water, unless it's a man and you're a woman and you're not really swimming, if you catch my meaning. Raising your arms over your head while you're pregnant can never, ever, ever strangle a baby with the umbilical cord, and, for the record, it doesn't matter how long you take a bath, you can't drown a baby who is already in water, even if it absolutely happened to your cousin's friend. She's confused, or she's a liar, and I am okay with saying that, because me and the facts—we're tight.

I love the facts so much that I dispense them to people who haven't even asked for them. I feel sure that knowing the details the way that I do will make you feel as calm as it does me. Does your baby cry in the evenings? To help protect them from predators, babies' temperatures naturally drop in the later hours of the day. The amount of fat in breast milk goes down then too— both actions designed to make your baby crabby and ask to be held in the evening, when predators are most active. As a parent, I find that to be a completely comforting piece of intelligence. Knowing that biology and science could explain why I couldn't put that eight pounds of humanity down long enough to go to the bathroom made it so much less likely that I would put the baby in a box and leave for Belize, but when I told my sister the same thing, she looked at me out of a sleep-deprived haze and screamed, "How does that solve my problem, crazy lady?!"

This urge to see the truth, to revel in its honesty, is compelling enough that I sometimes want to do it even though it might spoil a moment for other people. A gorgeous video was making the rounds on the Internet awhile ago. It was a heartachingly beautiful film of a newborn baby being bathed in the most tender and human way, and everyone on the mailing list it was sent to—mostly midwives, doulas, birth workers, and mothers—were all practically sobbing, struck by the sensitivity and vulnerability of this brand-new person, and were making secret, deep, and passionate pacts with themselves that they would bring more of that sacred intimacy to every birth they attended. I was too, as I sat here with tears running down my face, and then I wrote back to the group to remind them that early bathing can actually wash off scent markers babies use to learn breastfeeding, and that it is ill advised to do so until the dyad is established. It was so touching.

This is who I am. Deeply rational, keenly analytical, and profoundly grounded in what is real and true and can be proven. I love to deal in what is completely, confidently factual. I love the scientific method. I enjoy research, and I thought that the class on interpreting statistics and studies I took in university was bloody brilliant. All this means I have no idea what it is about apocalypse movies that gets me not just to suspend all this but to buy into what they're selling completely. I know it's fiction, but if I told you the number of paperbacks I've tossed for having an implausible plot you wouldn't be able to imagine me gleefully queuing up a film that posits that a team of surveyors in the Arctic have triggered a global ice age with a big drill. Nope. I'll watch it, and I'll like it. A solar energy collection device isn't built right and creates magnetic tornados consisting of cars and muffin tins? Absolutely. They got all the cutlery too. Two teenagers become worldwide heroes of a potential apocalypse when a meteor strikes the earth, and they singlehandedly correct the flaw in the earth's axis with a laptop, their game console, and the battery from Grampa's old truck? I have three teenagers who can barely dress themselves and would be asking me to make them a sandwich for their escape, but somehow I have no problem with that plot.

It would appear that I am willing, in fact, to suspend any amount of reason, logic, and fact when it comes to meteors, instant ice ages, cruise ships struck by tsunamis, bizarrely localized lightning, and, indeed, metal tornados. If it ends or threatens life as we know it, I'm in, so my daughter Sam can be forgiven for suggesting I would love a movie in which a bizarre plague turns just about everyone on Earth into a zombie, who then threaten life as we know it. To her, it made total sense. I have a love for anything apocalyptic, and these zombies were, but I just couldn't do it, because zombies simply make no damn sense. In what could only be called a miracle of self-control for a teenager, Sam didn't say a single word about how the other film we were contemplating was a little gem called *Lava Storm*, but just asked me to elaborate.

My argument about zombies is that they are completely implausible. They can't work, I tell her, and my reasons are based on two facts and rules about how the world works. Fact the first: Decay is inevitable. If something dies, then nature reclaims it. Shouldn't zombies pretty quickly become, to put it delicately, "too far gone" to be any kind of real threat? In some of those movies, they're out in the sun for months, and the world just doesn't work that way with dead things. Sam took a moment and considered what I said and then reminded me that maybe zombies have their own rules. Perhaps, she hypothesized sagely, whatever made zombies into dead things that were ambulatory also made them things that didn't rot. I reminded her that were that true, zombies wouldn't be so disgusting. They'd look great, and in every movie I've ever seen I was somehow asked to believe that they'd decomposed enough to be scary and then somehow stopped at that point, just so they could keep terrorizing. That's totally preposterous.

Furthermore—and when I say "furthermore," you know I am about to make an excellent point—nothing on Earth can be alive without energy. Plants need water and nutrients, animals need food, everything needs something to eat or it starves to death, but here's a zombie movie where we're supposed to swallow the assertion that they're a huge problem months, or even years, after all the human food has got itself locked into a compound with a gun tower and ninety miles of razor wire. Why don't they starve and die off? "Mom," Sam had said, with none of the irritation in her voice that she was probably entitled to. "Zombies are dead or undead, or whatever. They're not alive, and they don't need to eat."

"Aha!" I say with the zeal of someone who is absolutely correct and hasn't been allowed to explain how just yet. "But it isn't just living things that need fuel to work. If your cell phone runs out of juice, it stops working. Cars are dead or undead, or whatever, and if you don't put gas in them, they won't move. Things cannot move without energy; that's a rule of physics, and that's how Earth works, and that is why zombies are completely unfeasible. They can't be a real thing."

Sam stared at me, and something passed over her face that looked like exhaustion. She queued up the movie about the underground volcano that nobody knew about, the one that erupts, sending lava through the sewers of New York City, incinerating thousands as they travel on the subway, and she sighed deeply. When she turned to me, she had a look that I recognize from when I've had to explain about how there's no way possible that Bill Gates is keeping track of how often you forward a letter about a kid with leukemia. She said, "It doesn't matter if zombies are implausible or if you think they can't be a real thing." With a look that said she's going to enjoy a lot more films than I am over her lifetime, she stated: "Zombies actually aren't a real thing."

Sam was right to be exasperated with me. For a woman who loves for things to make sense, I wasn't making a ton. Why should I accept that, someday, we might have to restart the rotation of the earth's core? What do I think I know about nuclear power plants that makes a film with a title like *Nuclear Hurricane* something I'd dial into while listing the reasons that zombies are a stupid premise? I'm proud of being a clear thinker, so isn't it weird that I would like to watch anything with a plot as implausible as a meteor that might ignite the methane in our atmosphere? (That was a good one.) I don't think so. I think the attraction is that, to my way of thinking, each of those plots has a seed of truth in it, a tiny little anchor that my rational, factual self can hang the rest of the premise on. There are meteors, and there are volcanoes, and solar panels are a real thing, and they're actually pretty new, so is it so wrong to think that one could trigger a magnetic tornado that pulls everything metal into its path? Maybe, or maybe not, but it begins with a premise that I can extend if I have to. One perfect, solid fact that can be the foundation of my leap.

Unlike zombies. They just can't be possible.

Writer

I am a fairly traditional sort of writer. I am not groundbreaking, and, much to my personal comfort, no critic has ever called me avant-garde or radical. My path has been pretty average, for both a writer and an author. I toiled in anonymity until I got an agent, my agent sold my work to a publisher, and I've been in the traditional writer/publisher relationship ever since. They seek books, and I seek their approval and money. (I worry that I want my editor's approval more than the money, but I think that's pretty normal too.) I'm okay with being traditional, and it sort of suits me. I write, I think, I write some more. I knit in between—rather a lot, to be honest, because it helps me think, and because I was born a little overly curious, and while I think that's pretty normal for a writer too, the knitting helps to keep me from going through other peoples' bags when I get bored.

I worry that someday I'll run out of things to write about and have to get a job where it's mandatory to wear pants every day, and I worry that I'm ill equipped for that. I've been a writer and an author for almost ten years, as I pen this, and that's a long time to live this way. I worry that being allowed to decide what my workday looks like for this long has probably made me unemployable, and I always struggled in the workplace anyway. I am the sort of woman who has been missing a completely replaceable knob on my stove for seven years. I don't wear any color but brown on planes because of my talent for and helplessness to prevent coffee spills. It takes a lot of self-discipline to keep me from procrastinating (more than I do). I know who I am, and while I have spasms where I wonder what things would be like if I were groundbreaking or independent, I know the odds are pretty good that I'm not built for it. I'm lucky that I've been able to create work for myself that suits me this well. Oddly, I have always believed that this is how most authors feel, that this is work and a job, that it takes a lot of structure to get it done, and that we should stay focused so we don't have to get outside employment. I say "oddly" because I've recently realized that I have no evidence to support this theory. Speaking with other people who do this work is rare for me. I write from home, and while I wouldn't mind talking with other authors, there are none in my office, and not a single one has ever self-identified to me at the grocery store, which is really the only other place I frequent.

A while ago I got into a conversation with my friend Andy, and I was describing my daily discipline of work to him—the way I get up, make coffee, then nail myself, unwilling and bitter, to my desk until I meet the minimum word count that I've set for that day. (The number of words varies depending on where I am in a book cycle and how much panic I feel about it.) I go nowhere, I do nothing, not until this bare bones of writing is done for the day. If all goes well, the work that I begin with my coffee springboards into a day of writing, punctuated by laundry, walks, knitting, and general productivity. If all turns ill, if I don't make this minimum, the day dissolves into disinterested pecking at the keyboard, punctuated by desperately distracting phone calls to friends, dejected attempts to deal with my e-mail, and me, still at my desk at 10 P.M., wishing for release I cannot have—not until I meet the word count. If this continues past 10 P.M., then eventually I have to grant myself some small forgiveness, fork over the day to disappointment, and lie in bed swearing I will do better tomorrow, promising that this day was an exception, and pledging that tomorrow will be the beginning of a fresh new me who always, always meets her word counts and also bakes all her own bread. Without this rule and the soul-crushing deadlines it serves, I told my friend, I didn't think I would be a productive writer. Andy was surprised. I saw it on his face. He told me that he had supposed (as many nonwriters do) that writing is a release of the inner artist within, something that must be done—much more of a calling than a job—and that he thought I would love every minute of it enough that I would be driven to do it, even if I didn't get paid. I didn't say too much back to him. I didn't want to be the person who shattered his illusions. I probably would still write if I didn't get paid, but I certainly wouldn't write as much. I wouldn't be able to, what with the little time I would have left over from my job at the sheet metal factory. (I worked at a sheet metal factory for just under nine hours when I was seventeen. It was the worst job I've ever had to do. Every time I don't want to do what it takes to keep this job, I remember that one.) I mumbled something about discipline—deciding to write and then just doing it—being the biggest part of writing, and when he looked at me like I didn't know anything about being an author, I left it alone.

Seven years ago, at the insistence of another (nonwriter) friend, I went to several writer's groups. This was doomed for a bunch of reasons I didn't know about before I went to them, but also because I am an introvert, a watcher. I get material to write about by thinking and seeing and constructing hypotheses (usually crazy ones) about the people I'm watching—and sometimes the person I'm watching is me. This friend was insistent that writers needed other writers, not because she thought I was lonely, or that sitting in my office drinking coffee and knitting while I thought about writing was unhealthy and weird, but because she believed deeply that writers needed criticism, and discussion, and feedback. I reminded her that I have three daughters only recently passing out of adolescence, and that means I get lots of criticism and feedback on everything from my writing to my hair. I reminded her too that I keep a blog, an online journal where I write almost daily, and that Internet writing generates a ton of really immediate feedback—if you choose to call the almost daily e-mails about my use of ellipses "feedback." (I do.) She pressed on, arguing that wasn't it possible I would be a better writer if I discussed my writing with other writers? If one writer thinking about my writing was good, then wouldn't two writers putting their brains on it be better?

I know what she's talking about. I used to be a painter, and even now I am a textile artist, and the kind of collaboration that she's talking about is, generally speaking, good for art. A thousand times I have sat with my other knitter friends, laid out my materials in front of them, and described what sort of thing I would like to make. Absolutely without fail this process steers me closer to making the thing I want to make or at least identifies land mines that I hadn't considered. I'll say I want to make a blue sweater that flows and has a certain neckline, and there will be someone there who tells me that they've tried that and it didn't work the way they did it, or that it did work and it's bloody brilliant but that the way I'm intending to go about it is going to accidentally create a pouch on the front that looks like a third breast. The conversation—the collaboration—is, at a minimum, useful, and if I am very lucky and all the right people think about it exactly the right way, it can be nothing short of inspiring. Other people's ideas are good to have in that forum, but I've never wanted them for my writing. Still, these writer's groups exist, so while I don't like the idea, other writers must love it. I decided to try.

Now, I know there are probably some beautiful and inspired writer's groups, ones that work just the way my knitting ones do, but I didn't find them. I don't know what I was expecting, but whatever I thought might be there, wasn't. I don't know if I expected to find writers talking about the process of writing, of how they make decisions within an essay or chunk of writing, how they work through editing, or how you can tell if you're done or if your ending is any good. I thought they might be helping each other with the work, or making suggestions about why your particular essay was sucking harder than a Hoover. I think maybe I expected to find a room full of people to whom I could finally explain how it is that I know when a sentence is right, that when it is done it has a rhythm to it that I find pleasing. A drumbeat, a waltz, a sound and shape that have always told me, more than any grammar rule or editor, when I am done and when I have it, and whether there needs to be a comma there. I thought I would be able to talk to them about the crying. About sitting at your desk and feeling the hot, humid breath of a deadline on the back of your neck and writing terrible, terrible first drafts that you just had to stick with until you figured out what the hell was wrong with them. I thought they might talk about the self-loathing and the procrastination and the way that it feels when you write really badly, and how to come back from that. I thought they would be talking about writing. Instead, what I found was that these particular writers weren't really interested in talking about writing. Quite the opposite, actually. They wanted to talk about not writing, and why they were not writing, and why writing was so hard they didn't actually do it much, and then, oh then, there were the conversations about finding or waiting for your muse.

Now, I am loathe to admit this, because I believe that most people think I am tremendously nice, and the truth is that, like most of us, I think horrible things all the time that have to be put down like a lame horse or a political revolution, but I was appalled. The minute I heard the word "muse" my antennae went up, because these writers were actually waiting for one to turn up before they started writing, and in that minute I would know that this writer's group wasn't going to happen for me, at least not in a productive way. I can't truck with the subset of my kind who think that producing writing is a magical gift that is fueled by inspiration, or that the stories and books that they write waft in on the summer breeze and only those attuned to the intensely shamanistic art of what it means to be a writer can pull the gossamer threads of the story from the air. Nor do I think that writers need to suffer—although it often doesn't hurt, since some great stories have come out of suffering. (Remind me to tell you about the summer I spent eating macaroni with margarine because my crappy boyfriend kept spending all our money on movies. It's practically a poem.) I don't even think (although I would love to, if only for the sake of my slightly shoddy self-esteem) that writers are special or extra smart. Writers, in the humble estimation of this one, are a lot like plumbers, or accountants, or anybody with a skilled job who has to show up, figure out a problem, and then do their job—like, every day.

This is an unpopular opinion with some writers. If you want to see rage—seething, roiling rage that shimmers below the surface of a room with only civility to hold it in—I dare you to walk into a room full of this sort of writer and tell them there is no muse, or that if there is a muse, she's probably a drunken teenager in tight pants who really wants to party all the time and needs some boundaries set up right away if the two of you are going to stay in any kind of a relationship. Tell them that there is only showing up for your job and doing it or not, and that maybe they should try sitting at their desk and writing until it's done, because there is no other job in the world where you get to lie on the couch all day and then whimper to your spouse that it "just didn't happen today" and get a truckload of sympathy. (For the record, having been there and done that, what their spouse is giving them when they tearfully confide that they didn't quite make it to the desk today is resentment masquerading as sympathy. There's only so long a spouse can reroute this successfully, especially if they're showing up for their job every day.) Hell, if you're a writer, staggering to your desk and writing something bad totally counts as writing. Rewriting counts as writing, editing counts as writing, but lying there waiting for your muse, drinking coffee at a cafe while you complain that you're not inspired, or attempting to snatch prose from the air (while eating nachos and watching *Coronation Street*) is not writing. I know, man. I know that writing has days like that, but I don't believe that, overall, writers are possessed of a skill that— unlike any other human talent—can come and go as the wind does, some days gracing you with the ability to be good with words and some days not. Writers can go long stretches without producing anything of value or coming up with a brilliant idea, but I truly believe that if you show up for work and try to do your job, the odds that you will produce good writing are much, much higher than they are if you're lying on the couch hoping to write that day or spending a lot of time talking to other writers about how you sincerely hope your writing happens really soon.

Now, if you are the daring sort, say such things out loud to a group of that sort of writer. I can tell you that three of them will get a gleam in their eye that speaks to the consideration of violence, four will burst into tears, and two will light cigarettes and tell you (perhaps drunkenly) that you have absolutely no idea what it's like to be a writer. (I will let you imagine how I have come to these statistics.) I am a writer, and I can imagine what it's like, and in that moment I wondered about the difference between "writer" and "author," the distinction being that the latter has been published. Was that the difference between me and them? I was the sole author in the group, and while not all writers are authors, all authors are writers, and it seemed to me that we should have had more in common. Did the difference in our attitudes have anything to do with the difference in our titles? Was I an author because of my approach? I sure wanted to think so, but it didn't seem like a conversation you could have with a writer who was weeping softly into a large glass of bourbon and telling you how writing was just impossible for her and how tragic that was on account of she was going to die if she didn't write.

My uncle Tupper once told me that the arts are strange. That in most other professions or industries there were benchmarks and standards that a person had to reach before they could declare a profession. You could not, for example, just haul off and start telling someone you were an electrician. You had to go to electrician school or at the very least have done a convincing amount of electrical work that met the housing code and didn't burn anything to the ground. If you just installed a new outlet in the kitchen because the one in there has always been dodgy and you're tired of wiggling the toaster plug to make it work, you're not an electrician, even if you are really proud. Not so in the arts. If you want to be a painter, you just paint. If you want to be a writer, you just write. Stephen King? Mark Twain? Their profession is writer, and I, a pale, insignificant shadow of them, get to list writer as my occupation too. As bizarre as it seems, insane even, this whole writer's group totally has the title too. (The first hint is that it was listed as "Writer's Group.") You don't have to be published to be a writer. The very good (or absolutely horrific) novel you've just written that will never make it to an editor's desk or a bookstore shelf—it's still a book. Writers get the title just from performing the action, and as I realized that, I realized my point.

I'm not going to believe those guys are writers. Not until I see them actually writing.

A Late Guy

My husband is chronically late. He's not horrifically late, but he's a little bit late for just about everything, just about every day, for any possible reason. We have a semiannual fight about his lateness, and it always goes exactly the same way. I point out that he's late. For the sake of accuracy and winning fights, you will understand that I choose to tell him this immediately after he is late, while the lateness is both fresh and obvious. Joe then tells me that he is not late and I am out of my mind. It just so happens that I am not out of my mind, and he is late, so I reiterate the point about the lateness. Joe again denies that he is late, and this usually propels me to my next point in the argument, when I say something like, "You are always late and never on time."

As an aside, I don't want to recommend my technique to everyone. It's not super effective and probably shouldn't be imported to your relationships. Saying "always" and "never" usually just triggers the other person to give you true details about the one time that they weren't late or did take out the recycling, and even if that time was twenty-six years ago, and their dad helped them do it, and it didn't go super well, it destroys your credibility. "Always" and "never" can derail a perfectly good marital spat that you're probably getting close to perfecting. I can only say those two words to Joe because he doesn't have a typical response. Instead of dwelling on the times that Joe has been on time (which he could absolutely do—he's chronically late, not a jerk), Joe damns the torpedoes and makes the same statement every time. He will insist, with great emphasis and emotion, that he is never late and always on time.

It is hard for me to explain what happens next. You would think that I could describe it with great accuracy, what with the amazing number of times it's gone down exactly the same way, but there's something about rage that blocks recall. I know that I sputter a lot. I know I tell him that he doesn't get to say he's not late when he's late this much. I know that if there are witnesses, I call upon them to testify to his lateness. I also cite previous times when he was late with a great deal of detail, because the amazing thing about rage is that while it does make what happened hazy to you later on, it gives you the gift of absolute recall during the fight. I'd describe it more, but it's like every other standard-issue repeat fight that most people have in happy and long marriages. There's always one topic that comes up over and over and over again. It's usually not something big, because not being able to resolve something big can be terminal to a marriage, but there will be one topic on which the two people can't get traction, such as cups up versus cups down in the cupboard, whether or not her mother should be allowed to enter without knocking, how much ice cream kids should be allowed to eat, or whether the cat should be allowed outside. Those fights are as perennial as the grass. They are fights about a difference of opinion, and it's fair (if somewhat annoying) to argue about whose opinion is more valid, and it's bound to happen when both people are right but disagree about that.

This is not what happens in our fight. When Joe and I have The Late Fight (it has a name), we are not having a difference of opinion. There's a set of facts. We have a reality in which there is a set time to arrive and Joe is not arriving at that set time. That is the technical definition of late, and he fits it. Given this truth, with Joe and a plan and a clock all in the same room, one would think that Joe wouldn't have a leg to stand on, wouldn't one? One would be wrong. Not only will Joe argue that he is not late, with the clear reality in front of him, he will do so strongly and emotionally. He'll say that he's never late, and he'll say it in a tone that tells me his feelings are really quite hurt that I would think that he was. He'll say that he is not that kind of person, that the sort of person who is late is inconsiderate, and do I really think he's inconsiderate? Is that who I think he is? Some kind of inconsiderate, late person?

Usually The Late Fight stops right there. Joe might be chronically late, but he's not inconsiderate. Not at all. He's actually a super nice guy, beloved by all, and revered by many other husbands for his prowess and skill in the field. He is kind and funny and gentle and . . . late. The amazing thing is that he doesn't think so, and it is hard for me to stand there and hurt him by saying things about him that he really doesn't believe. Hard, but not impossible, because I am not yet perfect, and I can admit that—and I don't mind telling you that The Late Fight only usually stops there. Usually I look at his face, see that he really, truly believes that he has never been late and that he would never be late, and I am able to stop. Sometimes, though . . . sometimes I can't. Sometimes I am compelled by a force within me to tell Joe things that he needs to know, right that minute. I remind him that his lateness was mentioned at our wedding, and it got a big laugh. I tell him that laugh was recognition. I point out that he never heard the national anthem at the kids' school because he always arrived for concerts just after it happened. I've been known to ask him if he's ever heard the national anthem—because, ya' know, they do it first everywhere. I say (sometimes with our children nodding alongside) that I am not the only one who thinks he is late. I tell him we all think he's late. That we talk about it. That we practically have a support group. That he is so late that we are all thinking about getting T-shirts that read, "I waited for Joe."

The whole time, Joe is nothing but wounded. Now, Joe is late, but he's not stupid. He can tell time, and he doesn't (typically) live in a house of lies and denial. He's a smart guy, and it took me years and years and years to figure out what's happening, how there can be universal consensus from everyone who knows him that he is absolutely, totally, without a doubt, regularly and completely late, and how Joe can look us all in the eye with the honesty that is so typical of him and tell us that he has absolutely no idea how we could ever think that. It turns out that it's all in the definition of "late," and once you understand the way Joe thinks of lateness and the exceptions to lateness that make you not late, you're there.

How about this scenario: One Sunday night, I asked Joe what time he had to leave in the morning. He told me, confidently, that he must leave at nine, as he had to be in the studio by nine thirty. The next morning, Joe was still drinking coffee in his jammies at nine fifteen, and, because I am me, I said something along the lines of, "Aren't you going to be late?" Joe being Joe, he said that he was certainly not going to be late. I'm still me, so I did something obnoxious, like remind a full-grown man that it takes thirty minutes to get to work, and that you can't go to work in your pajamas, and that, therefore, he was not only already late but was making himself later by the minute. Joe, still being Joe, looked at the clock, realized that this was more or less true, and then said he was not going to be late, and he could tell me this because he just now changed the time that he had to be there . . . in his head.

To my way of thinking, if you're planning on being there at nine thirty, and you realize that you're not going to be there at nine thirty but more like ten, and you recognize that, then you're thirty minutes late when you arrive at ten. Enter the miraculous mind of my husband now, in which, when you realize that you're not going to be there at the set time, you just change it. No problem. Your arrival time is now ten, you are not late (you are not even the sort of person who would be), and even though you hadn't told anyone that you changed the time in your head, you're not late, and they should trust that about you.

It took me some time to learn too that if you're standing on a corner waiting for Joe, and you've agreed to meet him at 10:00, and it is now 10:20 or 10:22 when he pulls up, and if, say, you were to point out the discrepancy between the time you were expecting him and the time that it is now—presuming, of course, that this mismatch would make Joe rather technically late—then you would, very likely, be incorrect, depending on the reason for lateness. It's also taken me years to figure out that Joe is not late if the reason that he is late is not his fault. For example, if Joe leaves on time to come home, but on the way there he is caught in traffic, and this makes him arrive later than he intended, he is not late. He didn't leave late, he didn't expect the traffic, and there was no way he could be in charge of the traffic, so therefore, since he kept his part of the bargain—leaving on time—he is not late, because his intention was to arrive on time. Get it? Similarly, if we're meeting at a concert and Joe arrives outside the hall on time but as he is parking the car he receives a phone call and takes that call and ends up coming to his seat a full seventeen minutes into the Brandenburg Concertos, he is not late. He arrived at the location at the expected time, he just didn't come in, so he wasn't late. He was there.

It turns out that to Joe's way of thinking, he is only ever late if his arrival is delayed by complete and total negligence on his part, unmoderated by the influence of others. If he intends to be on time but makes a decision to change his arrival time when things don't look good, he's not late, because he moved the target. If he has resolved to be somewhere at a certain time but the universe throws barriers such as traffic, phone calls, or conversations with neighbors in his way, he can hardly be responsible for that.

Lateness, it turns out, is not a state related to the clock, or the expectations of others, or how long they might stand in the rain desperately shielding a cardboard box with a melting ice cream cake in it. Lateness is an intention, a choice, and what kind of a jerk makes that choice? Not my Joe. He's not like that.

Let Me Get the Duster

My sister Erin is a lot of fun. If you spent fifteen minutes with her at a party, the minute you and I were walking away together, you would say something like, "Oh, Stephanie, your sister is so much fun." You'd be right too. Erin operates on a level that I can't understand, because I'm not fun like that, but I know people sure like it. Erin is so much fun that everyone we know has an Erin story, and she's the only person I know who has ever been kicked out of Graceland by someone who was laughing. She invents games like family DJ, which was such a smash hit last Christmas that it almost topped the year she pretended not to know her skirt was tucked into her panty hose the entire holiday. People smile when they say her name, because she is genuinely, outstandingly fun to be around. Erin is so fun that it is an act of cruelty for her to stand next to me, so much does it accentuate the absence of fun within me. Not too long ago, we were at a party together, and I looked over to see Erin standing on a chair, pretending it was a stage, using a rolled-up napkin as a microphone, and dancing and lip-synching to a completely ridiculous song she had no right knowing the words to. Everyone was screaming with laughter, and I turned to my mum, who was standing beside me laughing, and said, "Erin is so fun."

I think my mother heard a tinge of jealousy. I've always had a thing about my sister. She's a lot to live up to. Erin is the kind of beautiful that means that when I am with her, men approach me all the time, but only to ask me if she is single and if I can introduce them to her. (In a few low moments, I may have been slightly less than honest about her marital status. I'm not perfect.) I wouldn't mind so much if Erin and I could just be the kind of sisters where there's a smart one and a pretty one, but she's not an idiot, and I can't tell you how disappointing that is to me. My mother knows all this, and so when I said that Erin was fun, my mother's knee-jerk reaction was to immediately say, "Oh, Stephie, you are too." Now, I am a humor writer. My job is to look at ordinary things and try to see how they are funny, and then write that down in a way that is funny, and doing this does something amazing to my reputation. It makes people think that because what I write is sometimes funny, then there are excellent odds that I am not just funny but that I'm going to be tons of fun, and I'm here to tell you that this is absolutely not true. I am funny, not fun, and there's a big difference.

Except for completely practical reasons, I have never stood on a chair, and if I'm on a chair, people aren't screaming with laughter. They're noticing how uncomfortable I look and saying things like, "Be careful you don't fall." I do make people laugh. I've done tons of shows where people laughed a lot, but what I say and do is almost always planned, written down. I can find that funny part of me while I am here writing, but the sort of wild abandon that Erin finds so easy and people find so fun is something that I can't connect with. I don't do abandon. I do concern. I do worry. I do overthinking. The last time I stood on a chair it was to change a lightbulb, and I spent the whole time realizing that, because I'm five feet tall, everything in my house above my sight line is filthy. I stood there trying to mentally calculate how many tall people had been in my house and seen the top of my fridge and generally marveled at the grime that existed above the sixty-inch mark. All I can think is that, if you're petite, you too should go stand on a chair right now and see your house the way tall people do. You probably should be dusting something, and that right there—that's the biggest difference between me and people who are like Erin. Even if I had been remotely considering leaping onto a chair for recreational purposes, I don't have enough abandon to pull it off. I think people like Erin get on that chair and enjoy the perspective, and I don't think they worry about dusting or falling at all.

Beyond my sister's knack for delighting people and my knack for figuring out how to get stains out of things and knitting really well, I think I've settled on there being one big point of difference between us. There's a moment when an idea runs through your head, or something occurs to you, or someone suggests abandoning good sense and getting off the beaten path to have a bit of fun, and it turns out that all the best fun involves a little risk, a little bending of the rules, even if the rule is just "be careful." In that moment, every person on Earth asks themselves the same question: "What could happen? What could the consequences of this action be?" and what your brain says in answer defines whether you are fun or funny. People like me can think instantly of what could happen. A thousand things could happen. The chair could break. You could accidentally step off, or dancing on a chair could be not funny, and instead of being the life of the party, people could still be talking about it weeks later, shaking their heads sadly and mumbling about what you must have been thinking. I could rip my pants. It could be the funniest thing ever, or it could be the first day of the part of my life where I need a wheelchair to get around. The possibilities are vivid and real to people like us, whereas Erin and her ilk, their brain replies with, "Who cares? Get on the chair. This time we're doing Madonna, and you're going to need to tighten your bra."

I used to think that fun people were brave when I'd see them doing something risky that I would have never had the nerve for, but now I think they're not. I've decided that it isn't that fun people have thought about what could happen and they're okay with it. They aren't ignoring the dangers. They just can't think of what those dangers might be. They're not really that fun. It's that they are suffering a failure of imagination.

I have no such flaw. I can imagine all the things that can go wrong, so when I'm on a plane, for example, I follow all the rules. The last time I flew and the flight attendant told me to shut off my phone, I did. I didn't turn it to airplane mode, I didn't mute it, I shut that thing off—all the way off—and I didn't even try to turn it back on again until I had express permission. I even shut off the Wi-Fi before I turned it off, so that when it turned back on there wouldn't be even a moment of violation as I searched for the setting. After takeoff, there was an announcement letting us know that it was okay to turn electronic devices back on, and so I waited for the flight attendant to pass me so I could double check. She seemed a little annoyed for a second, but then I told myself that she was probably just impressed with my concern for safety.

I listened to an audiobook for a while. (I always check to make sure the Wi-Fi hasn't accidentally turned itself back on, because I don't want to be reckless.) At some point toward the end of the flight, something happened. It just stopped. The screen was bright, but no matter what I touched on it, nothing happened. It was frozen, and even pushing the little button on the top to restart it didn't change anything. This was all seeming like nothing more than a big bummer when it hit me. Very soon, a little light was going to come on overhead, and then the flight attendant was going to get on the PA and tell us all to turn off our electronics, and I would not be able to comply.

Now, here is the difference between me and a person who is fun. As I realized that I was not going to be able to follow the rule, I asked myself that question everyone asks right before they break a rule or depart from the beaten path. A voice in my head asked, "What could happen?" and whatever part of me is responsible for imagining possibility said, "Are you serious? Do you have a pen? Here's a list: The signal from your phone could interfere with navigation. The plane could descend to discover that it is nowhere near the runway, the pilot won't be able to correct in time, and we could all die. Also, your phone's electronics will screw up the sensors in the cockpit that help them avoid turbulence. That lady behind you is going to get hit in the head with that guy's laptop, and then the flight attendant will careen down the aisle to administer first aid amongst all the chaos, and as she makes her way down the aisle, clinging seat to seat, she will be yelling, 'Who has their phone on?! For the love of God, who is doing this to us?!' How about maybe the signal from the phone will interfere with whatever thingy it is that keeps them from crashing into other planes in the sky. You won't shut off your phone, and five minutes later a tiny Cessna (filled with a young family, taking their newborn twins to see their dying grandmother for the first and last time) will be unseen by the malfunctioning proximity equipment on the plane and will have to veer wildly off to avoid a collision. Sadly, the pilot of the Cessna won't be able to control the craft after saving all of us, and the little plane will hurtle out of the sky. That heroic pilot and the little family will all be killed. Our plane will be spared, leaving you to live with the responsibility for their deaths all the days of your life. Or maybe nothing will happen. It could be okay. Your call."

Now, as remote as all of those possibilities are, you have to admit that they are still possibilities, and so as the flight attendant passed me, I shoved my phone under my leg. It wasn't time to shut it off, but I didn't want to raise myself as a suspect or panic anyone on the flight, considering what could happen next. When she couldn't see me anymore, I took my phone out and looked at the battery. The whole thing could be moot if I was going to run out of juice before we landed anyway. I looked at the battery time and the flight time and realized I was probably going to be in prison by sunset. If I lived.

As the hysteria built, it did occur to me to start wondering why the hell the TSA let me on a plane with a device that could endanger everyone if you can't shut it off. I blamed the airline, then myself, then whatever regulatory body should have been regulating me. I told myself that if I survived this I was going to write Barack Obama one hell of a letter. By now, I was pretty much nuts. I had to take deep breaths and let it out slowly, in a controlled way, and force my hands to unclench. I stayed calm and tried to analyze the situation, because you don't see James Bond freaking out, and he gets out of everything. One time when I was coming through security, this fourteen-year-old TSA agent took away my banana because he felt that the banana was (on the inside, under the peel) "a gel of more than four ounces." I didn't say anything at the time, because to do so would violate one of my most important rules, which is that I never argue with someone armed, but even with the profound respect I have for prudence, that one seemed sort of overly cautious.

As I recalled that, I thought about everything that I had seen people go through to get on that plane. There are so many precautions that if I only looked a little bit better naked, I'd suggest that we fly without clothes, just to speed things up. The TSA doesn't let me fly with the tiny scissors I use to cut yarn, and once, the small bottle of hand lotion that my mother had was practically treated like nitroglycerin wrapped in gunpowder. I was surprised they didn't call in a SWAT team to take her down and disarm her when they found it in her purse, and the more I thought about it, after using millimeter wave detection to scan me for anything that I might have positioned on (or in) my person that could possibly injure anyone, is it feasible that these are the guys who would let me and everyone else on this plane bring on board a device that could cause a plane crash? The phone can't be dangerous. If you can't have nail clippers, could you have something that posed a real risk of interfering with plane operations if you don't shut it off? There's no way that they're relying on passengers to prevent plane crashes. What if someone like my sister decided it would be fun to play three more rounds of solitaire for fun, even though the light was on?

I thought all of that through, but I still couldn't relax. There had to be a reason that the rule existed—something I hadn't thought of, something I didn't know about airplanes and what makes them work. There were still too many answers to the question of what could happen. I considered confessing to the flight attendant. I imagined ringing my call bell, and then discretely telling her about the problem. My instincts told me that if I did call her over, it would probably be one of those moments in my life when I confess a deep, deep concern, and then someone pats me on the shoulder as though I'm a lunatic who worries too much instead of someone who is just trying to respect the fact that I've been directed to follow a rule that's being presented as important and mandatory.

The plane began to descend, and I formulated a plan that I thought addressed all the logic and concerns. Considering that the TSA is pretty neurotic, things were probably going to be okay, but I still didn't know why this rule existed and was enforced, so I couldn't be too careful. I held my phone tightly in my hand, screen down so nobody could tell it was still on. (No reason to start a panic, if I could help it.) I wiggled my foot out of my boot and pushed the boot against the bottom of my seat, where I could reach it without taking off my seat belt, and then I decided that I was, rather unbelievably, going to trust the TSA to make decisions about what is dangerous on airplanes and what is not, and even though they have a rule about shutting off electronics, I was going to assume that they wouldn't let phones get onto planes if they could do any real harm, but I was going to be vigilant. If there was even a hint of trouble, I was going to enact my plan.

It turns out that there was not so much as a whisper of trouble on the way down. Not even a moment. Not a bump, not another plane on the horizon, not so much as a furrowed brow on the flight attendant, which was extraordinarily lucky, because if we had hit two seconds of turbulence I swear to God—and not one word of this is exaggeration—I would have been the demented knitter in seat 32K, the one who whipped off her shoe, lowered her tray table, and then beat the living snot out of an iPhone for no apparent reason, all while screaming "I will save you, I WILL SAVE YOU ALL!"

See, that's funny. It's totally funny now. As I write it down, I can see that it's so incredibly neurotic it can't be anything but funny. I mean, what sort of person sits there with a Blundstone hiking boot placed within reach and mentally calculates the most efficient way to smash their phone into oblivion to save the lives of imaginary infant twins so he or she doesn't have to live with the guilt of their deaths? Not someone who is fun, I tell you, but that story goes over like a house on fire when I tell it at parties, and it tricks people into thinking that I'm fun, and that we're all laughing together, the way you do with fun people, except they're laughing because I'm crazy, and my imagination is out of control, and people will slap me on the back and say, "Infant twins! Where do you get this stuff?!"

Mark Twain said that humor is tragedy plus time, and I think that's how it works for a lot of funny people. While it was happening to me, crashing a plane with my phone didn't seem funny. Fun people? They live in the moment, abandoning concern and trusting the universe. People who are funny? Stuff happens (or almost happens) to us all the time, and as a result of our enormous imaginations, it makes for great stories in a book, but it's hard to live through. It's the addition of time that makes it possible to see our reactions as anything other than completely bonkers. Anything could happen, and I can see that all the time, but I don't think my sister's imagination is on duty full time like that. I don't think she could be on that chair if she was seriously conceptualizing the broken spleen I think she's headed for.

If your imagination is big, you see it all. The good, the bad, anything that's possible, we're turning it over in our minds, and that means we'll be having a good time later, when we've thought it over, and when the plane crash didn't happen.

In the meantime, you should totally invite my sister to your party. She's fun.

I Love You, Walter

I can never remember a time when I have liked the dentist. From the time that I was little, I have regarded the entire profession with a certain wariness. Part of this stems from my general dislike for teeth. I would like to blame a sibling for this, one with a propensity for biting that probably shaped at least part of my loathing, but really, teeth just gross me out a little, and they make me nervous. They're breakable but vital, fragile but permanent . . . I've always felt that teeth were a generally poor arrangement for mouths, and don't even get me started on the way they fall out of little kids' heads. It's revolting. I dislike teeth so much that I only care for my own to minimize the chances that someone else will need to touch them, and I barely got through the years I had to play tooth fairy to my children. I'd sneak into the room with a trepidation that had been building since the kid in question showed me that one of her teeth was a wiggly goner. Right then I'd start worrying about what I'd have to do later. (I'd also start trying to think of someone I could pay to do it, but that never worked out.) I'd go in and grope around under the pillows, both hoping for and against contact. At the moment when I found the thing in my hand, I'd try to shove it into a tissue as quickly as possible, before the sound of my retching woke the child who was expecting not a parent who was disgusted to the point of nausea, but a dainty, shining fairy who so loves teeth that she collects them all. It made me bitter to leave a quarter for the privilege. I was pretty sure the Tooth Fairy had the second worst job in the world. The worst job in the world, I felt certain, was dentistry.

The disconnect between how I feel about teeth and how I imagine a dentist has to feel about teeth has made it difficult to have a relationship that is built on trust with anyone in the profession. Like most people, I believe that I'm pretty sane. I even have a fair amount of evidence to that effect. As a sane person, I feel that my position on teeth is sound. I can stretch my imagination to grasp that there are people who dislike them less, and I can even somehow imagine people who are neutral, but to actually arrange your life and study and devote your daily working hours to looking into other people's mouths and not just touching their teeth but fixing them when they're even yuckier than usual . . . I try, but I just can't believe in the sanity of anyone who would want or like that, and it's hard to trust a crazy person.

I know not everyone feels the way I do about going to the dentist. I have a friend who loves it. She finds it relaxing, and as the mother of young children, she appreciates the chance to lie down. Me? I think that dentistry might be a little bit easier if we could arrange for the whole visit to happen while I was upright. It would make me feel less vulnerable and more poised for escape should the whole thing take a turn for the worse. I feel sure that my friend didn't have orthodontics in the eighties, and let me tell you, she might feel differently about the whole tooth thing if she had. When I was young, I had bad teeth. I'm not a big woman, and I had teeth I hadn't even started to grow into yet. The end result was not a complete overbite, but my two eye teeth on the top were shoved forward by the abundance of pearly whites. This didn't bother me that much—or at least not enough to get braces and risk being called "brace face," "metal mouth," or "tinsel teeth." I'd seen the sort of abuse other kids had been subjected to, and besides, a dentist had recommended them, and even at fourteen I had a pretty good sense of what those people were about. I refused to consent to the braces until the day a kid named Simon called me "fang face," and then it was an almost instant decision.

I don't remember my orthodontist's name, but I do remember he liked teeth (strike one), said my sister's teeth were nicer than mine (strike two), and always called me "Chief" in what I believe was a pathetic attempt to cover for never bothering to learn my name. (Strike three, though he was out from the start.) That man was single-handedly responsible for solidifying my hatred of teeth and of people who like them. Not much of that was his fault, but I blame him anyway. I had big, clunky braces for years, horrible headgear that I wore strapped around my skull at night, elastics that sprang off my braces and out of my mouth at moments that seemed timed for their humiliation factor, and, worse than that, I had to have four teeth pulled to "make room" for the rest of them. I don't think they do that anymore, but they sure did then, and I still haven't forgiven him—or teeth—for instigating the ordeal.

My current dentist, let's call him Walter, mostly because that's his name, tries to understand all of this. I can tell when I look into his eyes that he can't figure out how I can hate teeth any more than I can figure out how he loves them. He's told me that he thinks dentistry is an art, not just a science, and that he loves fixing things and making them right again. As a concept, that resonates for me, and I can even agree that nobody wants to walk around with broken and hurting teeth. Despite not liking this whole scene, and having worked up a pretty good phobia about what he likes to do, I manage to consent to the occasional cleaning and repair. I sit in the chair, and the whole time I weep on the inside. Obviously, what with him being a dentist, I can't know what Walter is thinking, but I suspect that we could agree on this: We have a relationship barely built on trust, shored up with respect. I can't entirely trust him, because he's someone who wants to touch not just my teeth but any teeth that show up, indiscriminately, and I'm pretty sure he doesn't trust me because I am skittish, nervous, accusatory, and suspicious while I'm with him, and by now he must worry that one day he'll come at me with the little drill and I'll go completely bonkers. I don't blame him for this. That said, I can tell that he tries really, really hard to accept that my worldview is one in which he's part of an inexplicable, terrible truth. We live in a world where there are dentists, and they do help you, and we do need them, and Walter and I do our best to accept that we coexist in this world.

My relationship with Walter is marked by moments of great truth on my part and moments of incredulity on his. For example, I am worried that one time when Walter gives me the freezing shot he is going to miss the mark. He's going to somehow dive into the wrong spot with that needle and inject all the lidocaine into an artery, and the whole whack of it together is going to travel to my brain, and I am going to have a dental anesthetic embolism. Naturally, I will not survive. I am afraid of this not because I have ever heard of it happening or have read a story where someone died this way, but because one time after he gave me the needle and left the room I considered this possibility and was then pretty sure that I could feel it happening. Later, when I didn't actually die, I Googled the symptoms of an anesthetic embolism. I couldn't find out what it was with any real certainty, but I did find out that it might have the same symptoms as a panic attack.

The next time I went to the dentist, I confided to Walter that this was my fear. (Well, that and the concern that I will drown while lying on my back in his chair, or that I will sneeze and he will accidentally drill my mouth, or that he will discover that all of my teeth need to be pulled out or are about to fall out of their own accord and he is helpless to stop them.) I worry about a lot of things while I'm at the dentist, but they don't seem preventable, so I try to keep them to myself. The embolism seemed like something that Walter could prevent if only he knew. I confided my concern, told him that I wanted to live, and that as a result I wouldn't be having any more needles. Walter, who really, really is a nice man and a good dentist, despite his lack of suspicion toward his own kind, was very reassuring. He told me point blank that an anesthetic embolism is a made-up thing in my head. It was impossible on about six levels, all of which were concrete, unchanging, and certain. I pointed out that embolisms totally happen. They are not impossible, and, as a matter of fact, I have read in numerous books (and looked up on the Internet) all sorts of murder scenarios where air (which seems so much less lethal than anesthesia) is injected into the bloodstream and, voilà. Death. I was not, I maintained, someone who didn't have the facts.

These moments are the reasons Walter can't trust me. The man carefully and deliberately explained about seventeen things about anatomy; how much anesthetic he was putting in; that it was going nowhere near an artery, so that, even if he missed, it wasn't possible to hit an artery; and how, even if he did inject the whole thing into an artery, an "anesthetic embolism" has never existed and could never exist. (He's right. I Googled.) Furthermore, he reminded me, he had gone to school for this, and the education was rather extensive. This risk, he felt, was probably something they would have at least touched on in his years of dental education or the decades of practice since then. He explained it all, and he made good sense, and at the end of his explanation, the good, reasonable part of me that has respect for his job and training was sitting in that chair nodding and accepting that he was going to give me a needle, even while the part of my mind that feels responsible for my safety was just screaming that he was lying for no reason other than that he's a tooth toucher, and they're basically dishonest.

I could tell that Walter really believed what he was saying, and more important than that, I could tell that Walter really believed that I was nuts, so I let that reasonable part of me be in charge, decided it was as good a day to die as any, and let him do it. That particular roll of the dice turned out all right, and I felt really good and brave. I had tried to love Walter, but I couldn't. He and I had reached an uneasy peace hallmarked by suspicion and wariness, though the whole thing was almost derailed the day that my husband came home with a patient-of-the-week mug, and I was furious. If anyone is patient of the week, it's me.

This was the state of our union—me trying, him trying—when I was in the Dominican Republic on holiday and a huge chunk of one of my teeth fell off while I was flossing. It was like a nightmare. I was in the bathroom, just flossing, not doing anything risky, when the tooth just came apart and a piece fell out. The world slowed down as I carefully spat the huge bit out, marveled at how little it turned out to be, and then panicked. This scenario is more or less the actual start of a real nightmare that I've had for years, and it has never failed to wake me in sweaty terror. I've always secretly known that it was less of a nightmare and more of a premonition, and the minute that I realized that it was all really going to happen it was so overwhelming that I had to hold my breath for a minute.

The next thought was worse. I might need a dentist. I might need a dentist in a country where I don't speak Spanish and they don't speak English. That thought had me sitting down hard on the edge of the bed. Perhaps, I thought, perhaps Dominican dentists are less scary. Perhaps dentists in third-world countries have clarity, perhaps the scarcity makes it simple, perhaps . . . perhaps I could wait until I got home. I probed the tooth with my tongue and it exploded with pain. It's hard to know what hurt the most, my tooth or the reality I found myself in. I spent thirty minutes sitting on the edge of the bed, checking and rechecking to see if the tooth was still broken, still looking at the bit of it clutched in my fist, wondering if this was like

terrible accidents in which other parts of you have come off –
was I supposed to save it? I was still hysterical on the inside, but
over that thirty minutes I managed to invent several lies to tell
my rational self that made it possible to move forward without
crying in public.

First, I told myself that my sister had been to the tourist
clinic the day before and, although the small town we were staying in was quite poor, it had been clean, sensible, and had an
English-speaking receptionist who had helped Erin and the doctor with communication. I was certain the dentist would be like
that. Also, I decided to tell myself that all dentists were probably
the same—the Spanish word for dentist was just *dentista*, and
that alone appeared to be a sign that the fragile peace I'd reached
with Walter was trust that I should have been extending to all
dentists everywhere, and it was time to simply grow up and get
it together. Finally, I reminded myself that rum was impossibly
cheap in this country, and I would not rule out any measure
of liquid courage. I went, and in a horrible, backward sort of
improbable support, my daughter Amanda went with me.

The clinic was, as my sister had said, clean and appropriate, with the usual amount of doctor stuff hanging around. The
receptionist was pretty and young, and she did indeed speak
English, and as she started to take my questions about the
dentist, I noticed that her teeth were just about perfect. That
moment, standing there in the clinic waiting room, talking to

the receptionist with the perfect smile, thinking that the dentist must be all right for her to look like that, was the last moment of confidence there was to be. Over the next two minutes, I asked a few questions that I thought were pretty normal and got a few answers that weren't. I asked her when the dentist could help me, and she didn't know. I asked how much the dentist charged, and she said it was up to him—and he only took cash, and I would pay him, not her. It turns out he's not really part of the clinic; he just rents a room from them. No one was entirely clear on what he did, what it cost, or how long it would take. She told me all this while beaming those lovely teeth at me. I tried not to freak out. All of her statements would be bright red flags in Canada—a cash-only enterprise out of a rented room seques-tered within an otherwise reputable business? In Canada, you'd know you had less of a dentist and more of a massage parlor that offered the suspiciously named "manual release," but this was another country—a third-world country—and, as I had earlier pondered on the bus with a stranger's chicken in my lap, things were different here. I had decided to not interpret "different" as "professionally reprehensible" and sat quietly waiting my turn. My daughter eyed me suspiciously, thinking that I was likely going to go over the edge at any moment, recognizing the thin, tight line of my lips as a sign that the stress of containing my hysteria was wearing on me. After chanting "things are differ-ent, not bad, things are different, not bad," about eight times,

I leaned forward in my seat toward the receptionist and asked the dentist's name. I thought maybe if I could start thinking of him or her as a person, it might lower my heart rate. She didn't know it.

Sweat began to trickle down my back as I waited. I felt it go and then realized that, despite the Caribbean midday heat, I was feeling chilled, and my hands had started to tingle and go numb. (These are, by the way, the exact symptoms of an anesthetic embolism, or a panic attack, depending on your perspective and beliefs.) The door to the dentist's office opened, and a woman left. She looked to me like she had been crying, but Amanda said that I was projecting. An ordinary-looking man, slightly overweight and rumpled, moved to the doorway of the office and signaled to the receptionist without a word. She waved at me, pointed at him, and went back to her computer. I clutched at the edge of my skirt, drying my sweaty hands on the cotton in case I had to shake his hand, and stood up. Amanda touched my arm—a sweet thought that I know now was intended as something along the lines of, "everything is going to be okay, mum," but which, in the moment, I could only interpret as a terrifying gesture of farewell.

I entered the rented room, surveilling as I went. The center of the room held a more or less normal, if somewhat antiquated, dentist's chair. One of those creepy lights with handles was over the top. An ordinary side table held instruments laid out on a white paper towel with blue flowers on it, and the only sink in the room was embedded in a countertop. I didn't see soap.

I sat on the edge of the chair, unwilling to lie down and be vulnerable in that room until I absolutely had to. I gripped the old vinyl, one of my fingertips finding a crack. The dentist closed the door and turned to face me, smiling—for what purpose, I didn't know. He asked me something in Spanish. I looked over by the counter, hoping to find the English-speaking assistant like my sister had with the doctor the day before, but found nothing more than extra paper towels and maybe a bug, which I tried not to think about. "No hablo Español," I mumbled. "No entiendo." He tried again, this time in something that was almost English, or might pass for English, supplemented with the smattering of Spanish I possess. I'd looked up a few emergency words on the Internet. "Tooth" and "broken" were now part of my repertoire. I lay back, wondering if I should tell him which *diente* was *roto,* but while I was trying to figure out if I should speak to him at all, he saw the thing. "Aye, yi, yi," he said, and came at it with a metal pointy thing. A shimmer of terror washed from the top of my head down, and I'm sure I visibly shuddered, but he kept coming.

As he neared, I realized my mistake. I shouldn't have wasted time on "tooth" or "broken"—those were obvious things. Completely obvious. Why the hell would anyone head to a dentist while you were on vacation if it was not about a tooth or if the tooth was fine? I should have spent a few minutes working on, "Can you tell me a little about your education?" or even just, "Please don't hurt me." It was in that second, as I realized that all my Spanish was completely wrong for my purposes, that he hooked a finger into the side of my mouth and mimed a gaping maw. As I saw him open his mouth to show me I should open mine, it occurred to me that he wasn't wearing a mask. Two seconds later, I didn't much worry about the mask as I realized he wasn't wearing gloves either. Nausea began to roll up from my belly and lodged in my chest, making me gasp in a horrible way that I'm sure sounded like a cross between a belch and the beginnings of a scream. The dentist didn't even glance up.

After poking around for a few minutes, he explained that he was going to drill by showing me the drill and pushing a button on it to help me understand. "Temporal," he told me. "Temporal?" I asked, mixing up the words for "temporary" and "early" (*temprano*), and I was suddenly confused, thinking that he was telling me that it was too early to drill the tooth—which, frankly, was a heck of a relief. My adrenaline-flooded system saw a way out of the whole thing, and in a rush, I decided to leave and to only drink liquids until I could get home—whatever it took. As I started to get up, one of his meaty paws pressed my shoulder back into the chair, and the grim truth of the thing hit me. I contained a sob, lay back in the chair, and decided to cast my fate to the wind and let it take me.

Thirty seconds later, I learned that one thing I didn't have to worry about was an anesthetic embolism. I realized that as this—let's call him a dentist, just for now—began to drill my shattered tooth without any anesthetic at all, which would have been worse if I hadn't been distracted by the realization that there wasn't an autoclave in the room. The drilling was bad, but it would end. Hepatitis is forever, and I bet there were even things on the drill that were worse than that. My mind reeled. I wondered what he would do if I fainted, because I was starting to worry about either fainting or biting off one of his fingers when I bit down to bear the pain. Maybe, I thought, as the drilling finished and I watched him start to mix a white powder with a liquid, stirring them with a regular kitchen knife on a regular plate, maybe this was more of a problem than I thought. Maybe I'd been so confused, so upset, so used to not really trusting dentists, that I'd made a huge mistake. No assistant? No gloves? No mask—no freezing—maybe I'd suspended my instincts too much. Maybe I had become so accustomed to bad feelings about dental care that I had forgotten that there were surely supposed to be some standards. Maybe, I thought, as I watched him fix up this paste for my tooth, maybe any minute now the door was going to bust open, and there would be Walter's Dominican counterpart, standing in the doorway, gloves and mask in hand, and the skilled assistant beside him would shout something like, "Juan! How many times have we told you not to touch the doctor's things!" With that vision, a new idea began to take hold, not just the very real possibility that I was letting a very bad dentist drill into my teeth, but worse, maybe this guy wasn't a dentist at all.

I spent the rest of the "appointment" realizing that this was a very real possibility, that my very permanent teeth—the ones that are not going to grow back at all and can't heal from any insult I allowed this guy to inflict on them—those teeth were very likely being damaged right that minute by someone who had less information about my oral anatomy than I did. He did what he had to do, it ended, I shoved the cash at him, and Amanda and I went back to our rented apartment, where I had a gin and tonic pretty much the size of my head. I wasn't ready to talk about what had happened or the mixture of insult and shame that I felt because this had happened and because I had allowed it. The sense of violation and regret was only amplified by recalling the worst of it, the moment when, while the "dentist" was leaning over me with the drill, a drop of his sweat had fallen into my open mouth.

Have you ever read a book where one of the main characters has an affair, and instead of destroying their marriage, it drives the adulterous spouse back into the arms of their partner? You know the idea—the grass always looks greener on the other side of the fence, but after having scaled the thing and dropped down on that sod, it turns out that this grass doesn't pick up its

underwear either. Then, presumably, one reflects on the invest-
ment and love present in the marriage and looks at this new
grass and realizes it's just not worth it, not compared with what
you've nurtured for so long. This, of course, almost never happens. Usually one person has an affair, the other one finds out,
and then the cheater leaves for a shiny new thing, leaving the
faithful old spouse with three kids, a cat, and a washing machine
that leaks half of the time. The first possibility—the chance that
crossing the line could improve a relationship—almost never
happens, but this is exactly the gift that the Dominican maybe-
dentist gave me. All dentists, it turns out, were not the same,
and this experience created a sudden wave of love and faith in
the glory that was Walter. It shouldn't be a surprise that Walter
would come up on the winning side of an equation that didn't
include basic hygiene on one side of it, but it was a surprise to
me that I suddenly wanted to be with him. It is not that I was
surprised to discover that Walter was a good dentist—I always
knew that in the sense of his skill—but now I was considering
another possibility, perhaps something I'd never thought possible to exist. Walter was a morally good dentist.

When I got home, I went straight to Walter's office, and I
didn't say much. Neither did he. He didn't ask me the kinds
of questions that I thought he might. He fixed the tooth, and
except for the flash of horror that I saw cross his eyes when I
told him what had happened, Walter was professional, kind,

and sympathetic, and for the first time in our relationship I felt genuine gratitude to him for taking care of my teeth. Walter is a good dentist, not just in the sense of his skill, but because of his ethic, and we are going to be together forever now, not just because he has a mask and gloves, but because after he looked in my mouth he agreed quietly, and with great sincerity, that based on that filling, he didn't think that guy was a dentist either.

A Large Hurdle

I am not a sporty person. There, I've said it. From the time that I drew my first uncoordinated breath on this earth, I have been nothing short of a physical train wreck in the gross motor skills department. I am very good at sewing and embroidery, and I have lovely handwriting. I once tried making *pysanky*, that Ukrainian thing where you use a tiny little funnel to draw with wax on eggs then dip them in dye. I'm brilliant at it. I can even do *bandhani*, a crazy Indian form of resist-dyeing where tiny little knots are tied with thread to make patterns on fabric. No problem. I can knit with an elegance, grace, and strength of skill that parallels an Olympian. If knitting were an Olympic sport, then I would be hanging out with Michael Phelps. Something happened to me as I first took hold of life, as my cells began to divide and multiply and the universe smiled down and decided what talents I would possess. It completely and totally neglected gross motor skills. I am so uncoordinated that it's as if the day they were handing out physical prowess I was distracted at the fine motor skills wicket, probably by a knitting pattern, and missed out completely on whatever it is that lets people do standing-up things with their bodies.

I have always wanted to be good at sports—any kind of sport. I watch sports in person and on TV, and I see those men and women who seem so beautiful, and alien, and impossible, and I want to be like them. Not totally like them, you understand. I don't need to be the best, and I'm never going to be interested in dedicating my life to something that makes you sweaty, but I would like to be able to do simple things, like toss a ball to another human being with the general expectation that it will land somewhere near their vicinity, or catch something someone throws to me with something other than my face.

I'm afraid I have the wrong temperament for sports. I'm a bit of a coward, truth be told, and that's always held me back. It seems to me that people who are good at sports aren't as afraid of pain. You can tell from the grimaces on their faces and the blood on their outfits that they are getting hurt over and over and over again. That makes no sense to me. The part of being a human that drives you to inflict pain on yourself seems to be missing in me, other than when I try to meet a knitting deadline.

When I was sixteen years old, I tried to run the hurdles. I was a good runner—little and quick—and running was a skill cultivated out of necessity because of the relationship it has with fleeing. You can ask Wanda Borden of the seventh grade why I got so damn fast. She and Monica Stepe inspired the hell out of me by standing near this big rock on my way home and threatening to beat the snot out of me. I saw them, and I ran—fast. My cowardice is not just instinct, it is intelligence. I knew that getting pounded by Wanda was going to be more painful than running, and that Monica holding me down and calling me "brace face" with all the pretty girls watching was going to be humiliating on a level that couldn't even compare with the crappy things that sometimes happened while running, such as tripping on the curb and getting a grass stain on my pants.

Fleeing from danger was a fabulous motivator, and by the time I was in grade nine, I was pretty good at it. Phys ed was mandatory, and running track was the only way I could get through it. Running seemed so much safer than anything with a team. By then, I was so good at running away that I accidentally ran my way into some track competitions. This mostly worked out until the coach saw that I was decent at the one-hundred- and four-hundred-meter dash and suggested I try the hurdles for those same lengths. Now, in case you don't know what exactly the hurdles are, let me sum up the basic premise. A sane, reasonable, intelligent person runs full tilt at a large, solid, stationary object, and then, at the last minute, they leap over this large fence and keep running as fast as they can toward the next one. Run, jump, run, jump, with no goal other than that of doing it faster than anyone else. To me, it sounded like a crazy and insensible plan, like skiing, where a seemingly balanced person stands on smooth boards that are waxed to make them go faster (if you can even believe that) and then launches themselves down a snowy, tree-lined hill especially selected for its bumps. I can't pretend to understand it, then or now, but the important part of this story is that I showed up and tried to run the hurdles.

I stood at the starting line, poised to sprint, telling myself all manner of things. I told myself the things I usually said at the start of a race, such as, "Just run away from Wanda. This is just like Wanda," and when the whistle blew, I took off. I'd like to imagine that my blond hair blew out behind me in a flowing wave of pale amber and that the coach watched me as though I were a dream of movement and joy, but what really happened was that I ran like anyone in a panic does, and it was nothing like a dream. I streaked toward that hurdle with every intention of jumping it. I had practiced. I knew I could jump that high. I knew because I'd walked up to it a thousand times in the previous week and stepped awkwardly over it time and time again. It was not too big, and it was not too high. I'd watched my classmates jump the hurdles, and although I'd declined to attempt it until today, it seemed possible. Sporty, but possible. I wondered, as I ran full tilt toward that little fence, if I would go over it the way they did. I started to imagine myself coasting over, long front leg extended forward, my back leg tucked toward my bum, my stride long and elegant. I tried to see it in my mind. The coach called this visualization, and he said it was essential. I had never seen him jump a hurdle.

Usually in this sort of story there are two possible outcomes. Either the protagonist, which is hopefully me, rises and overcomes her fear and concern and learns that in perseverance and bravery there is hope and success as she flies over the hurdle, soaring to not just literal heights but spiritual ones. That, or the protagonist (again, that's me) suffers a crushing defeat, falls over the hurdle, possibly winds up with some sort of a broken dream and bone, and despite her suffering, it's possibly funny, and you are inspired by the little engine that couldn't. This is not that kind of story.

In this story, here's what happens: I run. I run toward the hurdles, and I am ready. I am so ready. I have visualized. I have thought about it. I have no particular aversion toward running the hurdles, but I'm not really keen on it either. As I get close to the red-and-white striped fence that—may I point out—would be called a barricade under any other circumstances, I reimagine the way I will stretch and leap over the thing. I am, I think to myself, little, light, and quick, and I have found my sport. The hurdle looms, and I think not just about the immediate and miraculous way that I am about to go over it but also how amazing it is that this is so magnificently symbolic. I am literally about to overcome a hurdle, and I am suddenly thrilled and amazed that I am going to do this . . . but then I didn't.

I didn't jump it. Now, you might be thinking that I crashed into it, or that I tried and failed, but what I mean is exactly what I said. I didn't jump it. I ran full tilt at the thing, timing my strides to land me the right way over, and when I got there, one second before I lifted my right leg to go up and over, I had a thought, and that thought was "This could hurt," and I stopped. I stopped dead. It was as if there was a force field in front of it. My left leg came down to anchor me, and I didn't swing my right leg forward. I used all the strength in my little body to stop my momentum and come to a perfect still stand, inches away from the hurdle. It was the opposite of jumping, and I couldn't have been more shocked that it happened.

The coach was pretty shocked too, and I spent the rest of my school year trying to turn myself into The Kind of Person Who Could Do It, but it turns out that I couldn't, and here's what I told Coach Wells then: I think there is something in me, some really smart part of me, that simply will not allow me to run as fast as I can at a stationary, solid object. Call it fear, call it caution, or call it self-preservation, but there is an element of my nature that cares a very great deal about my well-being, and until you can prove to me that it is more dangerous not to run at that thing, I'm not going to do it. Not unless someone will be saved if I jump the barricade, not unless there is a fireball screeching toward me and jumping the barricade will get me out of the way, not until a swarm of bees chases me over the barricade, not until Wanda freakin' Borden (which is the most perfect name for a bully ever) made it a better choice to be on the other side of it was I going to take the risk.

I know that this is supposed to be the part of the story where I say that I got over it or that I learned how little it ended up mattering to me. How I learned to love myself the way I am, or that I'm good at other things, and that I let go of the lifelong attempt to be good at something physical like that. That I found a way to feel graceful and easy in my body and leave behind the dream of being like a gazelle or a little mountain goat, or someone other people describe as sure-footed. I know that this is the moment where I'm supposed to tell you that I moved past all that into the dreamy world of self-actualization and acceptance, and now I really, really like myself, warts and all, but it's just not true. I still look at people who are physically brave, physically bold, and who are able to risk themselves for no reason other than that it feels good, and I think they are so beautiful and brave in a way that comes with skill and prowess, and I still wish that when they handed that out, that I had wandered over for a minute and gotten just enough to jump the hurdles.

Snap

This is my favorite picture of my grandmother. I have many, but this is the one I love the best. It is a black-and-white photo, probably taken in the seventies. She is standing in a doorway of a motel room wearing a two-piece bathing suit and a bathing cap, but the cap sits loosely on her head with the sides folded up, the straps untied and dangling at jaunty angles. She's one of the few women on Earth who look amazing in a bathing cap. She's barefoot, and she's leaning against the door frame, her left leg hiked up, her left foot braced against the opposite side of the jamb. Her left elbow is resting on that upraised knee, and her head lies in her hand. Her right arm is down, lying against her right leg, and her cigarette dangles there. She, Kathleen McPhee, is looking straight into the camera, right at the photographer. She is smiling. Not beaming or laughing, just smiling and happy and relaxed, and I don't know who took the picture, but I know she loved them. I know this because it's how she looked at me, and just seeing the picture makes me remember what it was like to be not just loved but adored completely.

She looks exactly, perfectly like I remember her, down to the tiniest detail. I can almost smell her when I look at this picture. When I was a kid, my family didn't have a lot of money. We had enough, for sure—it's not like we lived in poverty—but while all the basics were covered, vacations were rare, and my grandmother, Gramy, used to take us on what we thought were amazing vacations. She'd pick up the four of us and my mother, and we'd drive to a nearby town and stay in a motel. You wouldn't think that would be an amazing vacation, but I didn't have much to compare it with, and there was a pool at the motel. That made it practically Disneyland. I saw my gramy stand in the doorway of a motel just like that a thousand times, and I might even have been there when that picture was taken. I would have been sitting on one of those plastic chairs, blue-lipped and shivering from swimming for so long, wrapped in a towel, sunburned and happy and watching her, hoping someday I'd be so tall and beautiful and funny. This picture might even have been taken the time my brothers lit the motel on fire. (It was mostly an accident. Or at least that's our story, and we're sticking to it.)

Here's another photograph. My grandfather stands in front of a cake, ready to cut it, and my grandmother is beside him. They are both handsome, fit people, and my gramy has short hair in this one, and that tells me that I wasn't born yet. She used to tell me that she grew her hair so I could brush it. My gramy isn't facing the cake; instead, she's turned toward my grampa, the hand closest to the camera tenderly on the side of his face, her pinky resting on his neck, and she's kissing him. They both have their eyes closed. I can look at this, and I can tell you that, unequivocally, my grandparents adored each other. Their relationship was passionate and intense, and I remember seeing moments like this all the time. Tender, intimate moments, when I almost felt like I was catching them at being in love. I used to go to their house for weekends all the time when I was growing up, and occasionally my grandparents would fight, and I don't mean petty arguments over small things. Big, dramatic fights with raised voices and slamming doors, and you would think that would scare a kid, but it never did, because I got to see the dancing too. I'd be lying in my bed on a Sunday morning and I'd hear the radio downstairs, and I'd sneak down over the stairs and watch my grandparents. They'd be wearing their dressing gowns, their coffee cups sitting on the counter, and they would be waltzing in each other's arms, all smiles. It was the first time I'd seen a marriage like that, with anger and forgiveness and frustration and joy, and it helped shape my ideas about passion of all kinds. That's what I see in that picture.

I turn the page in the album, and here she is again. Her long, dark hair is pulled back into a low, loose bun, the way she wore it the whole time I knew her. In this picture, she is sitting on the edge of the couch, knees together, leaning forward to rest her chin on the back of one hand, elbows on her knees. The picture isn't that great, except for the twinkle in her eye. It's the only part in focus—her dark, sparkling eyes and the mischievous, good-natured smile. You can tell that she was a lot of fun—and she was. Every time I see this picture, I want to tell someone about the two of us accompanying my grampa on a business trip to Calgary. I got to fly on a plane, and I got to dress up, and I got to go in the swimming pool and hot tub of the Calgary Hilton. It was in a solarium on the roof, and we ate in a restaurant, and I was nine years old, and I just about died of elegance. That night, my gramy convinced me to pretend I was sick so we didn't have to go to the business meeting part, and after my grampa left, Gramy and I went down the hall of the hotel to the vending machines and bought all the junk we could carry. We tucked into bed and ate chips and chocolate and drank cream soda and watched *Top Hat*. It was my first exposure to Fred Astaire and Ginger Rogers, and my gramy said that she thought I could be a fine tap dancer—if I wanted to be. That evening stands out in my mind still as one of the grandest evenings I've ever had. It was made only more glorious by the look on my grandfather's face when he came back early to see how I was feeling and found us practicing for our movie debut. "Lighten up, Jim," was all she said to him.

In what was the first real heartbreak of my life, my grandmother died when I was thirteen. It was sudden and shocking, and nobody was even a little bit prepared. She was fifty-nine years old, and the day she died was the first time I had ever seen my mother shattered and my grandfather in pieces. It scared the hell out of me. We were all so wild with the grief it was as if a bird in the house was frantically trying to find a window and get out and instead was smashing into everything. My brother ran down the street and away, and we found him later, sobbing in the closet of our neighbor's house. His own closet wasn't far enough away from the ferocious thing. It was the first time any of us kids had really lost anyone or seen grief, and at thirteen, trying to understand that she was gone forever was almost impossible. She has stayed gone, though.

My daughters never met their great-grandmother, and I have already had my mother much, much longer than my mother had hers. A friend of our family once commented that dead people in our clan were "less dead" than people usually are, and in a way it's true. We talk about them, we tell stories about them, their pictures hang in our homes, and we point at them and talk about who they were and what they did. We're a family of storytellers, and these photos have been our illustrations, and our kids have all grown up knowing all our people as best as they can, even the dead ones. Any one of Kathleen McPhee's great-grandchildren can point at the picture of her standing in the doorway of the motel, wearing a bikini and smiling at them, and tell you that she loved to swim, and loved the sun, and that she used to take her grandchildren to motels. They can point at a picture of her in her garden and tell you that she loved dahlias and tiger lilies, and that there was lily of the valley all the way along the side of that house to the backyard, and that when it bloomed she would snip big handfuls to bring in the house and put everywhere. They know all about her, and while it doesn't make her less dead, it does anchor what we have left of her, and I wonder if that would have happened without all the pictures. I'm so grateful to have them. I'm grateful to every person who ever took a picture of her and, more than that, I'm grateful to her for letting them be taken.

I myself have a problem with being in pictures. I feel self-conscious and awkward, and I usually don't look great in them. I am one of the world's least photogenic people, not because of how I look, but because of how I am. I inherited it from my mother. We're big, active talkers, and we wave our hands around and make faces, and that sort of vibrant personality essentially makes for terrible pictures. In all pictures of me, my mouth is open, my eyes are looking the wrong way, I'm making some accidentally rude gesture, and usually I look crazy, mean, angry, or all three—and for this reason I avoid having my picture taken. I don't think I'm too unattractive to be photographed; I feel like I get misrepresented. Add to that that I'm our family's photographer, the person who always takes the pictures, and what you have is a dearth of photos of me.

There exists in the world one picture—just one—of me pregnant, even though I did it three times. There are no pictures of me nursing my children, even though I did so constantly for years at a time. There are many pictures of my kids in the park, but it looks like I didn't go. The beach, Christmas, christenings, weddings—I am under-represented in the extreme. I pop up in group shots or the occasional picture with my husband, but if someone who didn't know us was given our family pictures and asked what our story was, I'm sure they'd tell a tale of an adventurous father who raised his three daughters alone, with occasional help from some crazy, angry, mean lady who crops up at Christmas and when they went to Disneyland. You wouldn't even think I was the nanny. She'd be around way more.

The day I put all that together and then put together what the pictures of my grandmother have meant to our family, I cried, and I deeply regret that I can't go back. Not for me, but for my kids and grandkids, and I feel like I haven't done my part in a family that keeps people around with their stories and pictures. I want for there to be pictures of me. I want for my daughters to tell their daughters the way I was, and it's not because I don't want to be forgotten, it's because it's easier to be without someone forever if you can invoke them at will, and that's what our pictures do. I don't want to take that from my girls—not any more than I already have.

I've started looking at my grandmother's pictures even more often, now with an appraising eye. She doesn't look awesome in all of them, not if you don't love her, but I do, and so I hadn't noticed the messy hair, the bathing cap askew, the hole in her pants. I hadn't noticed the messy kitchen behind her, the weeds growing in the garden next to the dahlia she's showing off, and I really hadn't noticed anything at all about what she was wearing or if her clothes were neat. I did notice that she was looking into the camera most of the time, and I wondered, since she was at least as expressive as I am, if she came up with a system for not looking crazy or mean in pictures. I noticed all that, and then I came up with a plan. It's got three parts, and it's really working pretty well.

First, I've stopped running when I see the camera. I don't duck out of the pictures, and I don't say, "Oh no, not now, I look awful." I don't tell people to put their cameras away, and I've stopped deliberately standing behind tall people. Second, I've come up with a system to look a little less wild in pictures and improve the odds that it will be a good shot. Now, when I see a camera, I stop moving, I turn to face it, I smile, and—this is the really important part—I stop talking. I close my mouth and I wait for the picture and, you know, I'm still not photogenic, but it's better. I think I've got it down to just one crazy eye now, and if I figure out how to time my blinks, I know I can get rid of that too.

Finally, the third thing. I still take lots and lots of pictures of all the people I love. I'm still the family photographer, and I love that role a lot. Someone took all those pictures of my grandmother for me to have now, and I like the idea that I'm doing that, and you couldn't pay me to stop, so I just changed one little thing. After I take the pictures, I pass the camera to someone, and I say, "Hold on. Take one of me." One of me in my garden. One of me with my nephew, one of me with my mother and my daughters and my husband and my knitting and the piano and on the beach, and when they take it, I look right into the camera, and I smile at my daughters and my granddaughters, and I show them who I am. Someday it will matter, and I've already lost enough time.

It's Not Personal

My husband and I have raised three girls. I feel like I could just stop there and get your respect, but let me tell you this: We raised three teenaged girls in a very small house with one bathroom and no shower. I imagine this means that someday I'll be given a special award for negotiation and creativity within the field of parenting. I imagine that when I am given this award, I will smile, bow, and then wave them toward my husband, Joe, because if anyone got us through the teenaged years without one of us ending up in prison, it would be him.

I'm putting myself on the list of people who were spared incarceration through that time because it turns out that I am not at all suited to being the mother of teenagers. I was great when they were tiny. I love rocking and nursing. I like talking to toddlers and watching people learn to read, and, besides, having banana in my hair never really spoiled my look. I've never had one.

When my eldest was born, everything went well for the first little bit, and I thought that I had given birth to an ordinary human child. Unfortunately, after she'd been on Earth about twelve minutes, she decided that she didn't like it much and proceeded to scream about it for several months. This is the story I tell myself. Other people say she had colic. My sister thought she was possessed by a demon, and my mother thought that I was probably just getting what I deserved for what I put her through, but I like my version best. This was, to put it bluntly, a terrible time, and at first I took it personally. Maybe my baby didn't like me. Her little eyes, slitted and hostile, and her face purple with her perfect, incandescent rage, and her hands balled into tiny fists all seemed to say so. She didn't sleep, she nursed every few hours for as few minutes as her survival necessitated, and the rest of the time she screamed, or, at the very least, complained. I tried every trick in every parenting book I could find; none of them worked, and I felt inadequate until, finally, I noticed that nobody could calm her. My mother tried, my sister tried, my friends tried, the midwife tried, our family doctor tried. One day, when my mother was desperately trying to soothe this wretched ball of seething humanity— rocking, bouncing, patting, singing "The White Cliffs of Dover" at the top of her lungs—I saw things clearly. It wasn't making a dent. The baby was still screaming, and I saw the look of savage, painful desperation on my mother's face, and it hit me. It wasn't personal. My baby certainly wasn't happy with her arrangements and felt that she was receiving substandard care, but it wasn't personal. She hated all of us equally. Relief washed over me, and from then on I approached parenting her with no less frustration but a lot less emotional pain.

This philosophy kept working for a few years. When, at age two, that same child developed a supernatural ability to get out of her clothes in public, I was mostly able to laugh it off. Maybe she was hot, I don't know, but the fact that she felt a deep and abiding need to be naked in the mall wasn't about me. Chasing a naked child was no fun, but I didn't think she was naked because she wanted to hurt me. Temper tantrums? Those were certainly not attempts to humiliate me in the grocery store. The kid (or kids, as the years went on) was hungry, tired, or stressed. They were not, I felt sure, doing this as a personal attack to make me unhappy just because the other mothers were watching. (On days when I was hungry, tired, or stressed, I absolutely was sure that it was a personal attack sent to make me unhappy but was usually able to right myself with coffee or a decently sized bottle of beer. I have no idea how people who drink neither survive parenting.)

This idea—this soft, warm idea—let me avoid most of that real pain in parenting that comes from taking it all personally, and it worked great until they were teens, and then the whole house of cards started to come down. At first, I was applying the same rules to teens that I used when they were little. Someone would have a screechingly rabid meltdown about homework or having to come home early, and I would take deep breaths and tell myself that it wasn't about me, that it was about a boy, or how crappy high school can be, or growing pains, or a burgeoning need for independence, or a big pimple right where everyone can see it, all of which are super upsetting. "Don't take this personally," I would say to myself. "You are not a bad mother. That is a bad pimple." The flaw in thinking that way is that something terrible happens to teenagers. I don't know what it is, although there were some very comforting chapters in some of the books, about them needing to reject their parents to become their own people, chapters I read over and over again while attempting to learn how to meditate and cultivate inner calm, but my whole system fell apart in the face of a fifteen-year-old girl who looked me in the eyes and said, "I hate you. You're a terrible mother—worse than all the other mothers, and this is completely personal."

I was suddenly adrift in a time where a girl would burst into tears about a pimple and I would be held personally and totally accountable for its presence. They'd break a rule, then tell me that it was necessary to do so because of my ridiculously restrictive rules. (I ask you now as I asked them then: Is wanting to be able to go into their bedroom without hip waders and a gas mask restrictive? I think not.) They'd sob about a complicated relationship, and I would say something like, "I'm so sorry this is happening to you," and they would look at me like I was born an adult and could have no idea at all what they were going through in any way. Worse, they were creative and intelligent, and while those things sound good, just stop to think about how much easier it would be to manage a slightly dim child who lacked the creativity to think up a good scheme. There were days when I wished I hadn't taken a prenatal vitamin when I was pregnant just to improve my odds of thwarting them. During this time, all of my best ideas for discipline turned out to be illegal. I wanted chastity belts, large cages built in the cellar, for the FBI to investigate every guy they liked, or perhaps just the legal right to sneak in while they slept and microchip them with a locator beacon.

While I floundered, Joe soared. He was suddenly and amazingly blessed with a miraculous and stunning ability to do the right thing and a profound certainty that they were pretty much amazing kids who would make great choices. If they broke up with a boy, he'd make twelve pots of tea, put on Aerosmith, and sit and listen to how sad the whole thing was while rubbing their backs. If they didn't do homework, Joe knew in his heart that they were the ones who were going to fail math, not him, and said so. He'd offer help, support, and the loan of his calculator, but make the problem theirs, not his. It was like watching a parenting ninja step out of the mist. This guy who had once accidentally thrown a baby into a ceiling fan (the baby was fine) and seriously contemplated giving a perfectly healthy five-year-old enough decongestant to knock her out for a little while, was now confident, creative, and thrilled to be parenting teenagers. He was kind, fair, and firm, and he innately grasped all the rules for parenting teens. Joe didn't sweat the small stuff, he gave kids ownership of their problems while remaining supportive, he was able to remember what it was like to be a teen and stay empathetic for how big and overwhelming the world was then, and he never once thought that a kid coming in twenty minutes late from orchestra practice meant they didn't understand responsibility and were probably going to drop out of high school. (That would be me, and, no, I never really relaxed later on.) In the face of what seemed to me like a frightening high-stakes game (which is totally how Joe felt about babies and little kids), Joe was relaxed. He laughed off blue hair and trashed bedrooms, and he just kept working his system.

If one of the magic ways through parenting children is to not take it personally, then my ninja husband discovered that one of the magic ways through adolescence is to make the other side of it neutral too. Their adolescent brains keep trying to hold someone else accountable for the stuff they're running on you, and that part of their brain is pretty sure that the discipline, correction, or conversation you're trying to inflict on them is nothing but an attack. The trick to our children's happiness turned out to be the same as the trick to mine. We had to find a way to make sure they didn't think what we were doing to them was personal either. That kid did not come in late to make you crazy, and at the same time you're not calmly telling them they'll be staying in for the weekend (while their mother builds that cage, because enough is enough) because you're trying to ruin their life either. Joe grasped this completely. Underwear on the floor? I was the shrieking harpy who wanted to know why they were so inconsiderate, thus provoking a fight with them because I didn't understand the pressures in their lives that made it impossible for their underwear to be anywhere else. Joe? He'd see the underwear on the floor and just say it was there, like an announcement. "There is underwear in the kitchen." He'd casually move on then, and nine times out of ten the offender would collect their unmentionables and quietly throw them on another floor somewhere else. (No system can overcome the basic nature of a teenager.) Joe strove for interventions that got him what he wanted without judging, arguing, or making it about anything to do with anybody specifically. You weren't a pig; there just happened to be underwear where we cook. It's about the underwear, not the kid. It wasn't personal.

Joe's greatest triumph, the pinnacle of his fathering career, was the invention of what we like to call "better parenting through nudity." It was inspired, and the idea arrived in Joe's head one morning as he emerged from the bathroom with only a towel, experienced a "wardrobe malfunction," and sent a teenaged girl screaming to her room in horror. His disgustingly decrepit and aged body (he was forty-four, or in teenager years, about a hundred and six) was, he had suddenly learned, powerfully horrific, and when you have teenagers, you take your advantages where you can find them, and Joe started thinking about that. With teenagers, your opponents are young, fast, and clever, and if you find something that gives you an edge, and if you can let go of the damage it does to your self-esteem, then you've got something. Something really useful. Joe saw the potential, and he ran with it.

The next night, Megan asked if it would be okay if a friend came over. We have long figured that it is better to have our kids' friends here than to have our kids at their friends' houses. It's cost us a lot in pizza and a fair bit of our sanity, but at least we have known where they were enough of the time that I stopped thinking it was a good idea to bungee cord their bedroom doors shut from the outside. We agreed that the friend could hang out until 9:30, because it was a school night. Predictably, at about 9:20, Meg made her play, asking for a little extra time. I was about to say no, that we'd made a plan and that she had a responsibility to stick to it, when Joe piped up and told her it was no problem. I turned to look at him and saw the twinkle in the eye of a man who thinks he's a genius. "Maddie can stay as long as she likes," Joe said to Megan, and I wondered if the strain had suddenly become too much. He continued, "Thing is, you should know that at 9:30 I am going to take off my pants."

The kid was out the door at 9:29.

Joe was thrilled with his new power. He was as a god walking the earth as man. The girls wanted to stay up a little later? Sure. They could stay up as long as they wanted. Hell, we could even have a family movie, all of us together in the living room . . . the only thing was that Joe was going to take off his pants. It was up to them, though. No pressure. They were gone in a flash. Your boyfriend is here and you'd like for him to hang out longer? Absolutely, kiddo, you should make up your own mind about that. Heaven knows that we recognize that you're old enough to decide for yourself. One thing, though. How does Josh feel about seeing Joe without pants? Not in the mood to go upstairs and clean your room? That's cool, but you should know that Joe's taking off his pants and cleaning up down here. It's all up to you. He had complete control, and he hadn't said "no" in a week. It was a miracle. It was everything the parenting books said it should be. Joe taking off his pants had nothing to do with them as people. It was completely free of judgment, it gave the teenager in question complete freedom to make a choice, and it respected their growing independence. It wasn't a threat; it wasn't even really discipline. It was just information, given from one person to another. It was just Joe saying, "I love you, and you and your sisters can do anything you think is right, but I am going to be taking off my pants. You can do whatever you want with that information. Peace out."

Configure This

I've been working on an amazing secret fantasy for a good long time now, and I've thought very carefully about whether or not to reveal it. I know that by writing it down here and making this deep desire public, I am removing my ability to ever actually make this fantasy a reality. I don't know if you've ever developed a really, really good plot, but if you ever do, it makes little sense to release the plan into the wild. At best, you expose yourself to the risk of plot theft, and, at worst, you lose plausible deniability. Think about it. If you were planning to murder someone, or at least have the option of murdering someone in the future, you would be a fool to openly say something like, "Bob? Are you kidding me? I hate Bob's stinking guts. I dream of having him to dinner so I can just get a little rat poison in his food." You'd be far wiser to say all sorts of complimentary things about Bob, about how amazing Bob is, and how you don't see why anyone could ever want to live in a world that didn't contain him. Then you murder him in a way that looks like an unexpected accident. The fact that you hadn't revealed your plan might at least slow the police down enough to let you make for Cuba.

Revealing that I think this way probably makes everyone I've ever effusively complimented a little nervous, and understandably so, but you see my point. I'm not planning to dispatch Bob; I'm just saying that if you're contemplating a crime, it's absolutely best to say nothing about it. Even fantastical plans that aren't quite crimes are best kept secret. There's always a chance that things won't work out the way you thought or that you'll be badly misunderstood. Choosing to keep my plans in my secret heart means that, when and if I do execute them, I can pretend they weren't plans but more like accidents, and I can't be blamed for those. All that said, I am still about to reveal a really good plot.

In my happiest dreams, the following happens. I come downstairs in the morning and limp into the kitchen to make coffee. While it brews, I tidy up the kitchen, as is my habit, and stare at my desk, working toward accepting that it and I will spend the rest of the morning together. The coffee machine eventually beeps, and I pour myself the first of many cups and go into my little office adjacent to the kitchen. I open my laptop, pull out my keyboard, and, as the computer wakes up, I note the time and make my daily commitment to my e-mail. I get a lot of e-mail, and I try hard to remember that I'm a writer, not an e-mail manager, because if I don't set a time limit for e-mail I can watch all my writing time swirl down a virtual toilet. On the other hand, I try hard to be a polite person, and that means I can't just delete something I don't have time to answer. I have to answer it, but I can't do that because I would end up spending the whole day answering e-mail, and, as I've already stated, that really can't be my life. A whole day spent answering e-mail turns into more days spent answering e-mail, because more comes in all the time, and when you respond to people's e-mails there's an excellent chance they will reply to your reply. Each e-mail I reply to is a potential seed of an electronic conversation with the possibility to expand into seventeen more e-mails. Admittedly, over the years, I've met many a fine person by way of e-mail. Some of my most interesting friends and peers came into my life because I took the time to respond to a random e-mail. The problem is that you don't know what sort of e-mail it is when it's just sitting there. You have to open it, read it, and process it to find out, and once you're doing that with all those e-mails, suddenly it's five thirty in the afternoon, you've had nine cups of tea, you don't know where your kids are, and you're trying to figure out why your editor is crying on a phone message about some sort of writing deadline—or maybe that's just me.

It turns out that I am not the sort of person who could possibly answer all of this e-mail—not without being poverty stricken or going to prison for child neglect—and it also turns out that I am not the sort of person who can commit to just dismissing an attempt by another person to communicate. These two truths are a trap. They mean that there is really no way I'm ever going to be able to deal with all of that e-mail, and, up until the plot I came up with, I only had one option. I had to pretend to myself and others that I was eventually going to answer them all.

For years, I wasn't just pretending. I actually believed that, as soon as I came up with the right strategy, I was going to answer them. I'd flag e-mails, and sort them, and write things like "answer e-mails" on Post-it Notes and affix them to my desk. I experimented with several grand schemes. I had an idea that if I figured out the average number of e-mails I received daily, then I could deal with that many plus ten, and that this would eventually have to have an impact on the tsunami of communication washing up in my inbox. That didn't work out very well, perhaps because how exactly I was going to "deal with" them remained undefined. It was always good for a few days, and then I would have a bad day when I didn't clear as many as I thought, or sometimes more e-mails would show up than I was expecting. Feeling that plan circling that drain, I would try to compensate by making the next day's e-mail load even higher, and pretty soon I was cheating. I'd tell myself that I'd amortize it out over a week, and that, sure, my performance on Tuesday and Wednesday had been weak, but wait and see—Thursday was going to be amazing. Thursday was going to be the day that I made up for Tuesday and Wednesday. That's right—Thursday I was going to do three times the amount of work I had found it impossible to achieve on any of the previous days. I have no idea what magic I thought was contained in that Thursday.

When that failed, I tried setting a minimum number of e-mails that I had to somehow magic out of my inbox per week. One way or another, through deletion, or answering, or whatever, I was going to have fewer e-mails in my inbox every single Monday in my future. I usually accomplished this by deleting junk e-mails, which meant that the first few Sunday nights went really well; but once I'd weeded out the flotsam there would be only real, meaty e-mails left, and Sunday would turn out a lot like those soul-crushing Thursdays. I tried a disastrous filter system that I read about in a magazine, designed to move e-mails of different types into different inboxes so that I didn't have them all in one spot. Looking back, I have no idea how that was supposed to work. Perhaps it was based on the idea of dividing an overwhelming job into bite-size pieces, or maybe it was to separate the e-mails so that they couldn't breed, but whatever was supposed to happen, it was an abject failure. At the end of the exercise, I had seven inboxes that were all completely out of control in every meaningful way. It was like touching a drop of mercury and watching it split into seven shimmering and impossible drops of quicksilver. I think I'd heard the word "filter" and had hoped the system worked like an actual filter, straining impurities and improving the quality of what got through, that somehow I would be able to filter out all the stupid e-mails, all the worthless e-mails, all the e-mails that said things like, "I am beginning to suspect that you only write books for the money," or that kindly inquired about whether or not I was concerned about the size of my nonexistent manhood.

One book I read about e-mail suggested applying corporate time-management skills like the "touch it once" principle. To make this work, all I had to do was vow that I would deal with each e-mail as it came in. This made sense to me. The minute I read any e-mail I would, I swore, either answer it, file it, or delete it. This was such a colossal failure that it made bathing a cat look easy. It didn't allow for the sort of e-mails that fell into whole other categories. It wasn't as simple as answer, file, or delete. What about the e-mails that demanded research before you could answer them? What if they were remarkable in some way and I needed to give them a little think before I could decide to answer? What if I knew it should be deleted but needed some time to reconcile myself to that? What if the e-mail was infuriating or ridiculously outrageous? What if it was so completely, infuriatingly, ridiculously outrageous that the only possible thing any person could ever do with it was read it out loud to two of their friends in the afternoon before deleting or printing it for framing? Wouldn't that e-mail have to be saved until at least then? I found exceptions to all the rules, and every inbox strategy failed like yo-yo dieting. I'd lose some inbox weight, then gain it all back, plus more.

Years ago, I was in Gros Morne National Park in Newfoundland. Up on a mountain in the Tablelands, there was a spot where so much snow had fallen, the summer hadn't been warm enough to melt it all away. The geologist on staff at the park made some comment about how maybe that tiny patch of snow was a baby glacier. It turns out that glaciers inch into being. Every winter, new snow falls on top of the old snow from the winter before, and unless the summer can melt it all away, layers upon layers accumulate. The weight of the newest snow compresses the older snow beneath into glacial ice. This, I realized, is what happens in my inbox. A communication glacier was forming, and everything that's true about a glacier is true of my inbox. New e-mail lands on top and the older e-mails become more compressed and immovable down at the bottom. The new e-mails are easiest to deal with, but the one near the bottom from about five years ago—from the woman who said that she would enjoy my books ever so much more if the publisher would stop putting my picture on them—that one is just about stuck. I'm still working on my answer, but the thinking on it is, frankly, also moving at a glacial pace. Even the metaphor of the calving of icebergs off of glaciers is appropriate, since that's what happens when I'm possessed of the will to take another run at getting control of my inbox. My effort lops off an iceberg of e-mail, cuts it adrift to float off to wherever dead e-mails go, but the glacier remains.

The glacier metaphor, though apt, is not reassuring. If my inbox is a glacier, what can I do about it? Won't it just keep growing and growing? As far as I know, the only threat to real glaciers is global climate change, and that isn't going to help me. If anything, climate change is probably going to make things worse, as concerned friends land e-mail after e-mail in my inbox, encouraging me to worry about it and recycle something else. (There is a lot of irony in knowing that the carbon footprint of the Internet—the thing that's creating my virtual glacier—is in the hundreds of millions of tons, which makes it a fairly significant contributor to the problems facing actual glaciers. Someday, I think, all the glaciers will be gone because of my e-mail, and we will have only my inbox to explain to little children what a glacier was like.)

I have tried hundreds of times to get my e-mail under control. I have tried different techniques, I have tried different rules, I have tried perseverance and willpower and deciding to be a different sort of person on Thursdays, and nothing has changed except that now there is more e-mail. There is just more e-mail coming in than I can make go away, and, layer upon layer, lo, a thing is being created, a thing that surges and retreats but is always there. I still try. One night, after a particularly bitter struggle with my e-mail, I decided to take advantage of the fact that, contained in the same computer as all that e-mail, there is the ability to search virtually all the knowledge of humanity.

Did you know that if you search "e-mail problems" that all that comes up is people who are having trouble getting more e-mail to arrive? People who can't receive it, can't access servers for it, can't send it, or can't reset passwords, or think that maybe their mail client is configured wrong. They're all trying to get more e-mail to come, not desperately trying to figure out how you deal with what is already there. As I scanned down the screen, all I could think was that I would love it if my client became unconfigured. I would laugh for an hour if my server stopped serving me more e-mail or if something broke like that; and, suddenly, the fantasy was born.

In this dream, I come downstairs. I make the coffee like I always do, and I sit at my desk like I always do, and when I open my e-mail I take a deep breath and look at what's there. Four thousand and twenty-six e-mails, all read, all filtered, all sent to different inboxes, all sitting there bloated and gleaming with the certainty that there is nothing at all that I can do to ever, ever get it all answered, and they are right. It is a task that is too big for me, and as I look at the list and scroll and click and take the measure of it all, a feeling comes over me and says, "Why do you feel like it's really important to spend this much time serving this system?"

That hit me like a ton of laundry. Am I sure I want to spend this much time serving this? What is this thing really? It's a system that allows people to reach me whenever they want. It's like throwing your front door open and welcoming in anyone who wants to come and promising them they will all get a grilled cheese sandwich, no matter what time they arrive or how well you know them. No matter how much you care, and no matter how much you want to give everyone a grilled cheese because you're nice like that, at some point you have to accept that you've made a mistake offering it. You look around and realize that your best friend and a bitchy colleague are now sandwiched between a woman who says her wallet was stolen while she was on vacation and just needs a quick loan and some guy who wants to know if you need cheap Canadian Viagra, and you've committed to getting them both a stinking hot sandwich, and how stupid was that?

In this dream, I realize that. A plan forms, and then something amazing happens. Tentatively, I put my hand on my computer mouse. I click on the first of my inboxes, the smallest one, and I click SELECT ALL. I take a deep breath, and then I delete them. All of them. Everything in that inbox. I wait for a minute, but nothing happens. No lightning strikes me, my phone doesn't ring—I don't even have the stomach cramps that are usually the physical manifestation of my guilt. Nothing happens at all, and, emboldened by that, I click on another box, and another one, and by the end I have done all of them. In the end, I have deleted every single e-mail that I ever possessed. All of them are gone; and while I sort of had worried that maybe there was something really important in there, it does not feel like that now. In this imagining, it feels light, and I hold my coffee cup in my hands, and I look at the empty inbox, and I can just feel the joy that is rising within me. I want to keep that feeling going, so without even thinking about it, I unconfigure my mail client. (I don't really know how to do that, but surely it isn't hard to look up.)

That's it. I have no e-mail, and more can't come. I giggle and start to think about what I can do with my day. The world is my oyster now that the e-mail is gone. Now that thinking about it is gone, and now that worrying about it is gone, why, I even have back the two seconds of my life that I spend thinking, "Oh bloody hell, there's another one," every time I hear the chime. I have a fresh start, and it feels like the day in 1993 when part of my stove broke and, even though I really love cooking for a herd of ravenous ingrates every day (who doesn't?), we had no choice but to eat in restaurants and get my favorite takeout for a week.

My plan needs the icing on the cake, so I imagine that I go to my website and put up an important notice for the world to see. The notice says that my computer broke. It really broke, and all my e-mails are gone. Every one of them. I think the server broke too, and maybe it was a virus, because it took out whatever it is that you're about to tell me is my backup thing too. That thing is dead as a doorknob. Dead like the computer the repair guy told me is no longer a computer, just an expensive aluminum brick. I would say that every single e-mail is gone, and that I'm simply devastated, and that this tragedy, the loss of every single word they have ever sent me (and are all waiting for me to answer), is almost more than I can bear. I would type that I am going to have to take at least a week to weep, to knit, and to try to recover from this, and that I know they will someday want to e-mail me again, but that I'm just not emotionally ready for that. I would try to write so it sounded as if I were crying.

Now, I know that if I were to do this I would be telling a lie, and I didn't miss the day of kindergarten when they said that lying is wrong. I know that executing this would be horrible, morally speaking. (Literally speaking, I actually think it would be pretty freaking awesome.) I know it would be uncaring, and you could probably throw in reckless, since I would be deleting several thousand e-mails and I wouldn't even know what they all said. Some of them could be important, or from people I really want to hear from or get to know. Trust me, I understand that as I reveal this magnificent, shining plot to murder my inbox and then lie and tell everyone that it fell down the stairs, I cannot impress upon you enough that I am not that person. I would never, ever do this.

I love my inbox; I think it's fabulous and essential. I love that chiming noise, and I would never want to live in a world without it; and besides, I couldn't write an essay like this and then kill my inbox. If it ends up dead, it was totally an accident.

Unusually Persistent
and Determined

You wouldn't think that a smell could wake you. Loud noises maybe, like thunderstorms or a raccoon knocking over your garbage and turning it into an urban buffet, but you wouldn't think that there would be anything that could smell bad enough to wake two people up out of a sound sleep; but if you thought that, you'd be wrong. The smell that suddenly permeated our entire home dragged Joe and me up from a deep sleep just about simultaneously.

It was summertime, and the smell of skunk wafted in, mingled with phlox. Actually, "wafted" is the wrong word. It was more like a smell truck slamming into the whole house. That first night, we thought a poor little skunk had been hit by a car or gotten into a fight with a feral cat right outside our door. The stench was so profound that we both woke up cursing, with our eyes stinging. It was so strong that I couldn't believe it wasn't visible. It should have been a fetid green vapor hanging in the air. The whole house was impregnated with it. In the morning,

Joe and I searched for the body outside, but there wasn't any evidence of the offender, alive or dead. We tried to air out the house by leaving the windows open wide.

This turned out to be a tactical error when we woke up the next night and, though we hadn't believed it could be possible, the reek was stronger. Worse, the next day we couldn't get the smell out of the house. Joe and I talked about how we had to be on a new skunk's route. Some skunk must have taken to walking by our house and spraying right in front of the place every single night. The smell clung to our clothes, our furniture. Fruitlessly, I bought an air freshener, but then the place just smelled like we'd been sprayed by a skunk that liked to roll in lilacs.

The third night, we were watching TV in our rank living room when our cat went bananas. She'd been sitting in the window, surveying all of her domain, when she saw something. She climbed the screen with her claws, doing an amazing impression of Spider-Man, and screamed at the top of her lungs in outrage when she couldn't get through it. Joe leapt up, ran to the window, and looked out just in time to see a little skunk slip under our porch. "Dammit!" Joe yelled, and then the smell hit us. Our eyes streamed, we gagged and choked, but we couldn't move away fast enough. It took us twenty minutes to untangle the cat from the curtains and window screen, and three baths didn't get the smell off of us, and I didn't have it in me to try and wash the cat.

The next day, we realized we needed a plan. The skunk had to go. The aroma was clinging to us all day. The children were being mocked at school, and Joe and I had both had people at work mention the smell. (At the time, I was working at a health center that served the homeless, amongst others, and when someone who doesn't have access to a shower thinks that your hygiene is worth mentioning, you've got a pretty big problem.) I Googled "deter skunk," but the only thing I found was a suggestion that I mix cayenne pepper with water and spray it around, and another page I found cautioned against that, since it can get in the skunk's eyes and blind them. That sounded mean, and there was no reason to hurt the beast, just send him on his way, and besides the cruelty, a blind, angry skunk sounded like it could be an even bigger problem. I found the City of Toronto's animal control line and gave them a call. It turns out that skunk invasion isn't really uncommon around here, and Brenda, the ACE (animal control expert) who took my call, was superconfident that the skunk could be gently persuaded to choose another home. She gave me a list of things that work, cautioned me against the cayenne pepper (reminding me that animal cruelty is illegal), and wished me luck. The list started with the easiest thing, so I started figuring out how to ask Joe to pee in the garden.

My brother James, who just happened to have popped over for coffee, listened to me read the list. He's a straightforward guy, the kind of guy who just cuts to the chase and sees the simplest solution first. He practically shaves with Occam's razor, and he was pretty amused by our plan—and by "amused" I mean that he thought we were complete idiots. I explained that skunks mark their territory the same way that other mammals do, not just with the reeking fetid stench of their spray (which, it turns out, may not just be for defense but also entertainment) but with urine, just like cats or dogs. Brenda the ACE had explained that if another, larger, more dangerous predator marked that territory, then the skunk was likely to decide that it was beaten and move on. My brother laughed out loud when I said that, for reasons related to pheromones and the relative ease with which a guy could pee in the garden, male pee was better. All Joe had to do was go outside, stand on the porch, and then turn the hose (figuratively speaking) onto the garden all around the skunk's front door. It made sense. I'd think about moving if someone started peeing in my house.

My brother was skeptical, and he told me he had a solution that was guaranteed to work, would work tonight, and all it would take was a six-pack and a shovel. He'd take the six-pack as payment, come back that night, and lurk there, sitting on the edge of the porch until the skunk emerged. One swift, sure blow with the back of the shovel, a bit of digging to dispose of the corpse, and, as he put it, "Bob's yer uncle." I imagined this, and not only did it sound murderous, but also stupid. The skunk was armed with a weapon more effective than a shovel, and I had visions of the mission ending in a scene involving a pissed-off skunk and a massive tomato juice purchase on my part—never mind what would happen if James was caught. I was pretty sure that I couldn't come up with a way to make it look like an accident. James wasn't worried about any of it. "It will be quick," he said, and he wasn't worried about the spray. The skunk would suspect nothing.

Joe and I didn't entertain this for a minute. We're vegetarians, and people who think that animals have a right to be here, and while this skunk's happiness was not super important to us at this point, hiring a hit man to take the life of a fellow mammal for the paltry price of a six-pack of beer wasn't exactly the sort of people we ever wanted to be. We're friendly, hippy folk. We felt sure that skunkicide was a bridge too far for us. Public urination seemed more like our style. Our house is in the city, and our front garden is only a few meters big, and four steps off our tiny porch is the sidewalk and all the traffic that comes with it. There wasn't going to be a subtle way to pee all over the front garden, but Joe did it anyway. He waited until cover of darkness, nipped out in a pair of gym pants so he could be efficient, and was back in a few minutes, looking prouder than he had a right to.

That night was a repeat of the others. If anything, the smell was worse. While we choked in our bedroom, setting up fans to try and blow the odor out, Joe wondered if all he'd done was issue a challenge, started a literal pissing contest that he didn't know how he could possibly win. He was back in the garden in the morning. Desperation had made him bolder, and he stood in the morning light, coffee cup in one hand, our pacifist weapon of choice in the other, doing his duty to protect our home.

After another night in the trenches (by now we had the windows shut tight and were stuffing damp rags under the doors like we were trying to keep out tear gas), we had a family meeting about what might be going wrong. Our daughter Meg, who was about twelve at the time, said she'd been thinking it through. If, she wondered, the man pee was supposed to scare the skunk off, maybe the problem was that Joe was a vegetarian. Perhaps the skunk smelled nothing but salad and tofu on him and had correctly figured that Joe shouldn't be considered a predator unless you're a carrot. We bought the six-pack of beer and gave my meat-eating brother a less heinous job. He joined Joe on the porch that evening. I stayed inside and thought about the tatters my life was in.

Carnivore urine turned out to be no more of a deterrent. That stinky little terrorist was stomping right by our olfactory warning every night and then delivering a stink bomb of his own that rivaled anything we could combat, not if the whole family abandoned the bathroom. I consulted the list from the ACE. The next step was to try putting a radio on the porch overnight, tuned to a talk station. The idea was that skunks are afraid of humans, and despite the fact that this one had moved in with humans, which should have tipped us off, hearing human voices chatting on the porch all evening was supposed to deter the little pest, and I supposed it might have worked, but that night, as the noxious and miasmic gas filled our house again, we realized the radio had been turned off. Joe thinks a neighbor did it to be helpful, thinking we'd forgotten, but I Googled whether or not skunks have the dexterity you'd need to flip the switch. (They do.)

Step three, according to Brenda the ACE, was to soak a rag in ammonia and then observe the skunk's hole, waiting for him to leave for the evening. Once he was out, we were to use a broom handle to shove the rag under the porch, into his hole. There was considerable debate over which one of us was going to crawl in the garden to do it, but Joe lost. That night, the smell reached new heights of offense, and it didn't seem as if the skunk was just living his life, doing his skunk thing. It was like he was spraying the windows and the doors in some vengeful display of superiority. It was like he took satisfaction in knowing what he was doing to us. There was no other explanation.

The next morning, when I opened the front door, our ammonia-soaked rag was there. It was right on the front step, dragged out of the hole and returned to us. I imagined the skunk carrying it up to the door in the night, enraged at our moxie, and laughing the way that skunks probably do. He'd probably started telling his friends about the pathetic humans who lived above his porch. I stood on the stoop and wept.

When I'd regained my composure, I called Brenda. She chuckled at the antics of our skunk and checked to make sure we'd done everything right. Had we peed in the garden? Had we peed enough? I told her the whole thing, with Joe shouting more information while I was on the phone. Yes, I told her. We had peed in the garden. Two men had peed in the garden. The garden had been peed in so much that I was never going to be comfortable weeding again, that's how much we'd peed in the garden. (From the living room, where he was washing down the windows with vinegar, desperate to take out the pervasive skunk smell, Joe shouted that he'd done it five times. At night and in the day. Joe had peed so much in the garden that the lady down the street had ignored him when he'd smiled at her the other morning.) Yes, we'd put the ammonia rag in the hole. Yes, we were sure it was ammonia—and now I was getting annoyed. We'd done everything right, and all we'd done so far was piss off the skunk. He was spraying more than ever, and, you know what, I didn't like the way Brenda was so concerned for his well-being.

Brenda decided that we had to move to DEFCON 2, an actual barrier to keep the skunk out. We were going to need a shovel (my heart leapt for a moment, but it was just for digging), a piece of chicken wire as wide and deep as the hole, plus twelve inches on the bottom. We'd fold the chicken wire so that the twelve-inch piece made a ninety-degree angle to the hole-covering part. There were two important things to remember, Brenda stressed. First, we absolutely had to make sure the skunk was out for a walk when we covered the hole. We wouldn't want to seal him in by accident and have the poor little guy starve in there. (I agreed with Brenda wholeheartedly, but I can quietly admit here that his death was starting to strike me as less tragic than it did her. I didn't want him to die in the hole, but only because I thought that might stink even more.) We committed to the surveillance. The second thing, Brenda said, was more interesting. Skunks, she stressed, have limits. They're only so committed to digging to get back in. A skunk will only dig down ten inches and ten inches out. Then they totally give up. Something in them says, "Enough!" and off they go. Since the chicken wire would go twelve inches down and twelve inches out, the skunk just wouldn't have the fortitude for the task.

Joe and I got our shovel (no longer as committed to its normal use) and cut the chicken wire to the right dimensions. Forces assembled, tools at the ready, we stood in the living room, peering into the night, waiting for evidence of egress.

We waited. We waited some more. It got later and later, and we both started to think that maybe the skunk was out. Maybe he had snuck out earlier for some kind of skunk meeting where they all got together to figure out how to get us to abandon our homes so they take over the whole neighborhood. Maybe, we thought, we should already be out there. It was midnight, and we figured he must be out—but, what if he wasn't? Misjudging could have terrible consequences. We could end up sealing him in, and neither of us thought we could just let him starve if we did, and the scenario of trying to undo the chicken wire while we tried to free an enraged skunk was too horrible to imagine. We decided constant vigilance was our only possible path.

Around 1:00 A.M., the lilies in front of the hole quavered, and Joe and I leapt to attention. The perpetrator emerged. He stomped two hosta plants, trampled a pansy, and hissed at the fire hydrant before wandering off down the street, bold as a bus. Joe and I watched him go, exchanged a look, and went to work. By 3:00 A.M., we had dug a hole twelve inches deep and twelve inches wide and had arranged the chicken wire solidly in place. We had a wall of wire covering the skunk's door and then extending out twelve inches from the wall—a full two inches past the skunk's limit. We'd screwed the covering firmly down, and we'd backfilled the hole, covering all the wire, and stepped it firmly into place. It wasn't the easiest job to do in the dark, it killed what was left of my lilies, and there was no denying that the garden smelled like the bathroom in a cheap gas station. The whole time, we were nervous that the skunk might come back and catch us at it. Around 2:30, a neighbor's cat emerged from a nearby bush and Joe and I both had a stroke. When we were done, we both had baths and fell into bed, exhausted, just in time for the smell to hit us and the sound of scratching and digging to commence. The skunk had returned. We didn't care. Listening to that little bastard try and fail was worth it. We imagined his impotent frustration and rage, and we liked it.

In the morning, Joe couldn't wait to see. I made coffee, because I wasn't meant for hole digging at 3:00 A.M., and despite the invigorating force of victory, I was exhausted. Joe's scream of vexation sent me running, but I knew before I got there. Joe stood in front of the garden, red-faced and infuriated, his newspaper clenched in his hand. I went to him. We held hands for a few minutes, taking strength in our love for each other. A few minutes later I was dialing Brenda while stomping up and down the sidewalk muttering, "ACE my ass," under my breath.

That phone call probably wasn't great for Brenda, and I don't know how I could have made it better, considering what the skunk had done. The chicken wire was still in place, the screws held fast, and the skunk had just dug down and then out as far as he had to in order to secure his domicile. He was in there. He was right back in there, and I was exactly as polite as a woman who has been living with a skunk for a week can be. While I was talking with her, Joe paced back and forth, asking what the hell Brenda's qualifications were anyway, and our youngest daughter came outside with a towel over her mouth and nose and asked if we were going to have a skunk forever. I asked Brenda if she grasped where we were at. I told her that we no longer cared if the skunk lived or died. I told her we couldn't take it anymore, and I think I might even have asked her why she lied to me. "Ten inches, Brenda. You told us the skunk didn't have it in him to dig more than ten inches."

"I don't know what to say," she said. "I've never heard of a skunk that will dig more than ten inches—never mind twelve. That's sort of impressive for the little guy. The other ACEs aren't going to believe it."

"Believe it," I said, and imagined four big skunks with bad attitudes taking up residence under her porch. Brenda sighed, and I could tell that she was frustrated with my lack of respect for the skunk.

"I don't know what to say," she boggled. "I don't know anything else that will work. You're going to have to call in professionals." I fell to my knees as tears filled my eyes. "There are professionals?" I gasped. There was a full minute of silence as I let go of my amazement that this was the point at which Brenda was mentioning that there were skunk-removal professionals. That's the sort of thing I would give people as an option right before I told them that their next step was a landscaping mission in the dead of night in a urine-soaked garden, but everyone is different. "Give me their number," I demanded, and she did.

"When you call," she added, just before we hung up, "tell them you have an unusually persistent and determined skunk."

I called the wildlife removal service. They were sympathetic, and they told me not to worry, they have a system. It was so expensive that all I could think about was what my brother would have done with that kind of money. What they were going to do, they said, was come to my house and install a one-way door that led to a cage. "Your skunk will be able to leave but not get back in," the guy assured me, and he sounded pretty proud of the technology. "Don't call it my skunk," I intoned. "He doesn't belong to me."

"Oh, yes, he does," the guy told me. "But once he's in the cage, we'll come back."

"Then you'll take him away?" I asked, and I thought I might cry.

"We certainly will, ma'am." I loved this guy. I mean that. In that instant, this guy who was going to come and take the skunk away was my favorite person. He could have asked me for anything and I would have given it to him, and I think Joe would have supported that decision.

"They're going to put the skunk in a cage and take it away!" I shouted, and a general cheer went up through the house. Joe slumped exhausted in his chair, and his body posture was that of a rescued man. Freed prisoners of war staggering out of the camps have looked less grateful than my husband did in that minute, and the children were thrilled. They started buzzing about how long it would take for the house to stop stinking and for the cat to be less deranged once the skunk was gone. "I love you," I said to the man on the phone.

"No problem, ma'am," he said. "I get that a lot. Now, once we take the skunk away, you'll have eight hours to occlude him. Now, we can do that for you, or you can do it yourselves."

"You do it," I said cheerfully. I didn't care about anything anymore. I didn't care about money, I didn't care about war or famine, I didn't care about which one of the children I was going to sell to pay for it, I just wanted the skunk gone, and I wanted my new best friend to make it happen. I did ask him why the "occlusion" had to happen in eight hours. In my mind, once the skunk was gone, there would be no rush. We could have a life again. Sure, it's a good idea to cover the hole up or put in nine miles of chicken wire and possibly a minefield so that no other skunk can ever do this to us again, but surely we could do that after we'd had a full night's sleep and a party.

He explained the devastating truth. It turns out that skunks (in addition to not being willing to dig more than ten inches) are also unable to change their stomping ground. A skunk has systems and patterns in place, and it knows its way around its own neighborhood. It knows where the food is, where the predators are, how to get water, and the very best porches to snuggle under, and it's not very adaptable. Shipping a skunk off to a new area isn't good for the skunk. "It's like if I dropped you off in Burma with no wallet," the guy said. "We can't relocate the skunks. They might die, and there's a bylaw against it."

The horrible truth started to hit me. The guy kept on explaining. I could hardly hear what he was saying, the blood was rushing through my ears so badly. It turned out that what this guy was going to do was trap the skunk in the cage and then throw a blanket over it to keep him from spraying. Then they'd take the skunk away, but only for eight hours. Those eight hours (the longest the city says you may incarcerate a skunk) would be spent digging the entire front garden up and putting a sturdier version of chicken wire down along the foundation and the edge of the porch and then outwards, away from the wall. Like Joe and I had done, although he promises it will be more than twelve inches, and it will need to be, because, at the end of the eight hours, they return the skunk.

"We'll drop your skunk off after dark," the guy said, and I couldn't believe what I was hearing.

"It's not my skunk," I repeated, but I could tell nobody believed that anymore.

The next day, two guys came and attached the one-way door and cage, and overnight, that cage came to contain our skunk. Our seething, choleric, apoplectic skunk. That night was like nothing we had ever lived before or care to live again. Over and over and over and over the skunk railed, sprayed, and sprayed again, but at the crack of dawn a pickup truck arrived and a guy tossed a blanket over the cage and took our skunk to "holding." Four other guys leapt from the truck, shovels in hands, clock ticking, and proceeded to destroy what was left of my garden. The wire grid went up, and it was attached with wicked huge anchors. They weren't fooling around. That screen went at least two feet down and two feet out. I went out periodically to make sure they knew what we were up against. A skunk ninja. A skunk of cunning ability and supernatural guile. An unusually persistent and determined skunk. They kept digging.

The "skunk occlusion system" was in place by dinnertime, and the family gathered in the living room to wait. At seven, the light dwindled. By eight it was dark and, right on cue, our skunk arrived home. The covered cage was placed on the sidewalk in front of the newly fortified porch and garden, and then one of the guys leaned out of the bed of the pickup, grabbed a corner of the blanket, and yelled, "Go!" The pickup took off, the blanket was yanked away as they made a break for it, and there was the skunk. He took one look at where he was, gave us a look that said he'd never, ever find forgiveness in his heart, and then stomped out of the cage, onto the sidewalk, then straight into the garden.

He was perplexed for a minute. He walked back and forth, and then he started to dig. He dug and he dug, only taking breaks to hiss and threaten the cherry tree, and then, finally, he gave up. I watched it come over him, and it was a beautiful thing. The defeated skunk stood there and looked right up at where we were in the window, and I swear to you that he nodded. He cocked his little head, and gave us a little look that said, "Well played, sirs," and then he turned, sprayed down the house one last time, and wandered straight over to our next door neighbor's and directly under their porch.

We watched him go. I had thought that when we finally saw him shift off, we would be happy. I thought that we would celebrate, and I thought it would be a relief. Maybe we would feel those things if we ever got the smell out of the house, but for that moment, all I felt was a deep sense of regret. This fight had been so long and so terrible, and had cost so much money and so much sanity, and it had all been so needless. There has to be a way, I reflected, that humans and animals can share cities without it being like this. There has to be a way that we can create space for them that doesn't leave them with no choice but to make our lives hell, and I suppose that, if push came to shove, I would wonder if we had been making the skunk's life hell too. I mean, what was it that was driving him to spray so much, if not for the fact that he was misplaced in an urban environment? I thought all of this over, and I thought over the

$498 bill from the skunk professionals, and I felt genuine pity for my neighbors. It was their skunk now, and I felt a certain neighborly responsibility. Their kids were little, their lives just beginning. They deserved to know what to do, how to end this before it even began. We squared our shoulders and headed over to talk to them.

Joe carried the six-pack. I got the shovel and my brother's phone number.

Protect the Face

Early in 2012, fueled by what I can only imagine were still-developing frontal cortexes in the student body and the unbridled glee the faculty must have felt when students organized something totally legal and then showed enthusiasm for it, the University of Alberta coordinated to try and break the Guinness World Record for the most number of people simultaneously playing a game of dodgeball. Unbelievably, the record was pretty high. To beat it, they had 4,979 students, alumni, and staff, and more than 1,250 balls, and, completely of their own free will, these people lined up opposed to each other, and then the whistle blew. It was like a war. It was horrific to watch, and it went on forever. Kids were running and screaming, and the balls were coming from every direction, and even just watching the film of it I had flashbacks to the nightmare that was so many phys ed classes I had in high school.

Not in my wildest imaginings could I ever have dreamed something like dodgeball on steroids—six hundred stippled, blood red balls hurled through the air, with me reliving the days when I was their only natural target. I practically shook as I watched the video, and I don't know who won, and I can't imagine, with the world record on the line and that many hard, vicious balls ripping through the air looking to connect with tender, young flesh, that it even mattered. When it was over, someone interviewed a few of the kids and asked them what they thought. Predictably, what with them having volunteered, most of the kids said something like, "Wow, amazing, that was crazy!" or "That was so much fun!" and then they asked my kid.

For the record, this kid is not actually my kid, but he definitely must be from a remote fork of my family tree, or a long lost cousin's son, or maybe my eggs were stolen from me and implanted in some woman in the west, because this kid resonated with me on a cellular level. As his peers whooped, high-fived, and celebrated their accomplishment in the background (and some received medical attention) this kid looked straight at the camera and was visibly shaken. He was a slight kid, fair of skin and hair, and he pushed his slightly foggy glasses up on his nose, wiped a sweaty hand through his hair, and then glanced wildly to the left and right as though he still thought a ball might be coming for him. His face was pale with blotches of bright pink color high on his cheeks, and a blazing red ball print shrieked on his arm. "That," he said, with a voice that broke slightly from stress as he flinched away from the sound of a ball hitting the ground, "That was actually really scary." It was the face of trauma. I believe that kid is never going to be the same.

I stared at that child, clearly ill suited to having things hurled at him, and in that moment I reaffirmed something that I have thought for my whole life: A sadistic gym teacher thought up dodgeball. One who really, really hated kids and was trapped in a job that he loathed, and somehow the only way he could enjoy anything about his pale existence was to invent a barbarous, ruthless excuse for a sport that teaches kids no values that I respect. I can just imagine the look on his face when he thought it up, the delight he took as he realized that he had actually found a way to force kids to hurt each other for his viewing pleasure. He must have been giddy when it caught on.

Now, I know all the arguments in favor of having kids play sports. Sports are amazing, and sports really benefit kids, and kids should really, really play sports, and I mostly agree. Kids who are engaged in sports are less likely to drop out, less likely to get into drugs, less likely to be obese, and less likely to fall pregnant—even the girls. Sports teach some kids all kinds of things, such as how to lose decently, how to win graciously, how to cooperate on a team, and how to tough things out. Sports, overall, are good, or mostly good for most kids, but I don't think that dodgeball fits in with what sports do for kids. I hate dodgeball, and it's not just because if I think about it for more than two seconds I can still feel the sting of the ball and imagine throwing up in the girls' locker room.

I've spent thousands of hours trying to turn a whack of little kids into individuals civilization can work with, and that means I've laid out the rules for them. We don't hit other people, we don't hurt people on purpose, we don't throw things at other people, we let other people take turns, we don't leave anyone out. I'm not the only one who says this stuff either. Show up on any playground and listen for a minute and all you'll hear is that message getting sent down the pipe to our young. We even have laws against some of the stuff that happens in dodgeball. If you're on the street and you haul off and throw something at another person with the intention of hitting them, you can expect the full weight of society to land on you, and mostly, we're going to call that assault—or give you time out, depending on your age and what you throw. Overall, in places where there are laws and rules, society has pretty much decided that it is wrong to celebrate the pain of others, never mind make it a goal, but here you have dodgeball.

Dodgeball is the only sport I can name where the violence or roughness of the thing isn't just incidental to the goal. Hockey and football are both activities where people occasionally end up hospitalized, and they can proudly boast that injuries are either wrong or the result of overexcitement or accidents, because the point of the game is to move a ball or puck from one side of the field of play to the other, but there are penalties for trying to hurt someone while you do it. Even in wrestling, an endeavor where two nearly naked humans grapple each other for physical superiority, there are rules against "unnecessary roughness." Not dodgeball. Dodgeball has one goal. Take this ball and try to hit that person over there with it. There isn't even a rule against aiming for your face.

The problems don't end there. In most sports, a kid can strive, improve, and lean on the team and hope for the best while they wait to get better, but not dodgeball. If you're not good at it, you're out. Ten seconds after the game starts, long before you would get a turn, or try to get some practice aiming a ball at another human, or even dodging it, for crying out loud, a ball comes screaming across and nails you, and it's over. You're on the bench until the next time you're declared a living target. In this "sport," people with crappy skills are eliminated straightaway, humiliated over and over again, and given no chance to get better, and, also, it can break their glasses. My grade ten gym teacher was a bitter, twisted human, and so we played dodgeball every rainy day for the better part of a year. I had lots of chances to play, and I can tell you that I never threw a dodgeball. I don't think I even touched one with my hands, except if it hit them while I was in a defensive posture. To this day, I can't tell you how I was supposed to get better at a sport where my part only lasted ten seconds, and it wasn't just me who was frustrated. It let down the other kids on my team whose odds of getting nailed by a ball went up every time I got laid out. That's not team building. It's just a way to make sure that the kids on your team eventually hate you as much as the opposing team does. I used to wish I could fake asthma so I could get out of it.

One day, my kid came home from school and told me that she was next on the firing line, that the allegedly safe place I was sending her to be educated had somehow decided that the rules of life and decency were going to be suspended for two hours a week while the "no hitting" rule the school had the rest of the time was going to be transformed into a permissible, psychotic kind of endorsed stoning, and the other kids were not only going to be allowed to hurt her, but encouraged to do so. I thought about what that does to kids, the look on the faces of the guys who threw the balls at me, and the way a whoop of joy went up when they hit me, the degree of volume commensurate with how hard the ball connected. I was only a teenager when I saw it happening, and I still knew a mob forming when I saw one. I looked at my kid, and then I wrote a note saying she wasn't allowed to play dodgeball on account of we're decent, law-abiding people, and also I think she sounds like she's getting asthma.

It's years later, and even the mention of dodgeball is enough to send shivers down my spine and make me want to plan some sort of mission where me and a riot squad of other mothers break into school after school and put a stop to it, on purely humanitarian grounds, and I want to be clear about my motives. It isn't that I disapprove of sports. It isn't that I sucked at it, and that it hurt. It wasn't about getting picked last for the team, and it wasn't even that it favored the brawny and punished the puny, because, to be brutally frank, most of us tiny kids were used to getting our arses handed to us at every sport anyway. Sports in general are like that. The kids who are already physically skilled have a way better time of it than those of us who are waiting to develop, or grow a little bigger, or be more coordinated, and most dorky kids are totally reconciled to their lot in the realm of physical education anyway. We might be a little sad from time to time, but we are used to a system that favors big, strong, physically mature, aggressive boys, and sets back those of us who were small, cautious thinkers who sometimes even lacked the advantage of a penis and liked to knit at recess. It's not that at all. It's that if I'm trying to raise nice people who don't like hurting each other, then this game makes no damn sense, and to quote my soul-kid, it's just too scary.

If you're a teenager who is ill suited to the rougher stuff, and tomorrow is your first day of dodgeball, I have some advice for you. Don't even try. There's no need to perfect any skills here since dodgeball has nothing to teach you. The best thing you can do is to let them hit you. Don't fight it, because maybe if you finesse it a bit you can at least pick the part of your body that the ball makes contact with. If you're little, or you're slow, they're going to be aiming at you. Protect your face and glasses, and try to ignore the look on the face of the kid aiming at you. He or she is not really like that—it's just dodgeball rage. When the ball connects, go sit on a bench and remember a bunch of stuff. Remember this game is inexplicable in the face of what your society values and what they want from you as a kid. This lapse is temporary. An hour from now, the "no hitting" rule will be back, and it's really okay, and even preferable, for you to live your ethics every minute of your life. Some of our most amazing thinkers and doers have been people who wouldn't compromise on violence. Finally, remember that, no matter what happens in that gym tomorrow, someday you'll be an adult, and they can't make you do this then.

An Open Letter to the Media re Unrealistic Portrayal of Life

Screw you. There, I've just come out and said it, and now I feel ever so much better. I've finally come to the conclusion that every single marketing attempt ever directed to me was designed to make me feel absolutely inadequate, and that it's not by accident. I'm not stupid—I get that the whole idea of advertising is to make me feel like my life would be better if I bought whatever product you're hawking, but do you need to set the bar on life so high that no person could ever reach it? Every time I watch a commercial and see family life represented, I feel the way I did when I found out that only about 6 percent of six-week-old babies sleep through the night. That's almost none of them, but I can't tell you how many people used to ask me if my babies were sleeping through and then frown at me when I said they weren't. Years later, what do I find out? That it's normal for them to wake up. Totally normal, and that made me feel terrible at the time, and now I just want all the time I spent defending my normal babies back. I was totally doing it right, and there was no reason to feel bad, and that's how all your commercials make me feel. Like normal families are continuously pleasant, thin, good-looking, preternaturally calm, and living in homes where you could lick any surface, anytime. Realistically, do you have any idea how many families have clean floors? Not that many, or maybe just the 6 percent whose babies are sleeping at night, but you've got spotlessly clean floors in all those ads, just like it's normal, and you're killing me.

When my first child was born, someone gave me a framed poster for the nursery, or rather the room of the crappy little apartment we'd decided to put the baby in, which, I guess, made it a nursery automatically. This poster was lovely. It was a blissful mother cradling her contented infant, both wearing full, flowing white nightgowns, standing in what really is a nursery in front of a window through which sunbeams were falling to warm them both with glorious, peaceful light. The baby was sweetly chubby, the mother surprisingly thin, and together they were greeting another peaceful and beautiful day.

That painting hung in my "nursery" for about three months before the afternoon that I finally smashed it into the garbage bin and walked away sobbing. Not once had my baby and I had a morning like that. Not once, and I was furious, because, you know what? That poster was trying to make me feel like maybe it wasn't going very well, and maybe I sucked at it, and that was not true. That poster didn't know what normal was. I really liked being a mother, and I thought I was pretty good at it. My baby was clean and growing and she cried a lot, but some babies do, and I'd totally figured out how to cope with all that. I'd figured out how to deal with the fact that something was frequently leaking out of some part of my body that wasn't usually all that leaky, and I'd even figured out what to do if you start to leak milk in the grocery store and it's not the kind in your cart. I'd accepted that I wasn't ever going to sleep through the night again, and for the most part, I was cool with that. I understood that little babies have needs and I had agreed to meet them, and, in a miracle of humanity, I didn't even find that sad. I was enjoying life as a parent and had accepted that there was always going to be puke on my shirt. That's the best you can hope for at three months, and that poster held out an ideal that wasn't just hard to meet, it was impossible. There was no puke on that mother anywhere.

That poster wasn't all. Everything that you've ever tried to sell me has represented an absolute joke. For example, that children's cold medicine? I saw your ad for that, and in it you had a sad-looking mom and kid, and then she gave the kid your medicine, and in the next shot the kid is up and around and running through the house happy and completely well. Do you have any idea what kind of hope a commercial like that holds out to a parent who's been locked in the house for three days with a kid who's bitchy, sick, and 50 percent full of snot? We all understand it isn't going to work that way, and we all know that maybe you're going to be able to make that kid just 30 percent full of snot, but the kid is still not going to be able to go to school, and that means that we're taking another day off, and maybe you have a job where your boss is down with that, but I don't know why you'd want to take people completely on the edge and imply to us that a product is going to deliver us anything remotely like that. (As a footnote, "non-drowsy" is not a selling point for most parents. The kid's sick, tired, and horrible, and last night they couldn't sleep because they were too busy puking on the hall carpet. Sedating them isn't really something we're looking to avoid anymore. I think I speak for many of us when I say it's a goal.)

While I'm on a roll, let's talk about how you're selling me paper towels. When my kid rips through the kitchen and knocks something over, I don't tilt my head, put my hands on my hips, and smile at their youthful exuberance before rushing to grab a roll of toweling so that I can have the special joy of cleaning up after the ingrates. Mopping up crap they spilled is not fun, no normal person enjoys it, and I'm not looking to raise a bunch of terrors who think that it's my job to make their world tidy. I'm going to call that kid back into the kitchen, ask them to slow down because they're breaking stuff, and then hand them a paper towel on the off chance that I can eventually teach the wildebeests how to be responsible adults who can clean up after themselves. I think that's what most parents are after. You know, the paper towels aren't your only problem here. Only drunk mothers smile endearingly when they find that their little Picasso has written on the new paint job in the hall, and what those teenagers did to the kitchen is criminal, not another awesome opportunity for me to fulfill my need to wipe things down.

It's like you have no idea what's really going on, like you've never met a normal family. Here are a few tips. My living room doesn't look like that, my kids aren't that clean, and I don't need to know how to get wine stains out of a white carpet, because I'm normal. I'm not stupid enough to have three kids and white carpet. I swapped out for brown years ago because it's the color of coffee, dirt, and the excrement of most mammals. What I really need to know is if your product takes out the smell of cat pee, because my seven-year-old was playing some kind of "lion in a cage game" and accidentally trapped our aging and angry cat under a laundry basket in the living room for two hours, and the cat served up justice the way that cats do best. When I see you showing me a family with a white carpet, I just wonder why you're shoving this in my face. Can you comprehend that, for most families, a white carpet means the only two beverages allowed in that house are water and milk? Do you even get that?

When my kids were little, I was part of a rotating playgroup. Every week, we would meet at another person's house, and every time it was my turn I would have a complete and total nervous breakdown trying to get the house clean enough to have the other mothers in. The whole thing was pointless, desperate, and a complete sham. Half of the time I ended up putting all of the dirty dishes in the oven, all the filthy clothes in the closets, and clearing up messes by ramming them into laundry baskets that I hid in the basement temporarily. Usually I'd be crying. Then the mothers would arrive, and they'd say, "Oh, your place is always so clean," and I'd thank them. One day, while I was cleaning up for one of these things (and by cleaning up, you should know that I mean I was piling all of the paperwork that had accumulated by the computer into the middle of a tablecloth to more easily put it under my bed), my mother was visiting. She watched me for a while, and then she said something profound that's really stayed with me. It was, "Christ, you're mean."

She went on to explain that she thought that what I was doing was really, really crappy to the other mothers. I was going to do all this, to hide the way my house really was and what normal really looked like, and then they were going to show up and say what they always did about how impressed they were, and then they'd go home and look around their own house and try to figure out how I could do it and they couldn't. They'd stand there, looking at everything wild all around them, and they'd figure that they were just incompetent and abnormal. They'd think that, somehow, I could have three little kids and be an apparently good mother who read stories and played Legos and made a decent dinner and washed cloth diapers and still had a house that was sparkling, and they couldn't. I imagined them lying in their beds at night and thinking about my house, and promising to do better tomorrow. It broke my heart a little, but, to be fair, I told my mother, their houses weren't trashed. Their houses were spotless! I'd seen them when it was their turn to host playgroup. My mum looked at me for a minute like she'd seen shrubbery with more intellect than I had, and said, "Did you look in their ovens?"

I made a decision then. It's one it took me a while to get comfortable with, but I decided that I was going to stop faking it. I was going to stop working so hard to make all the other mothers feel crappy, and I was going to start showing them that I couldn't do it all. I started revealing what our normal was. I did it slowly at first, owning up to the fact that the kitchen was trashed because the baby was crabby and I spent the day rocking her instead. When the laundry wasn't done, I explained that it was because we'd gone on an adventure to try and see a snake in the park. We didn't find any, but it took all day. Eventually, the whole thing got more comfortable for me, and the other mothers relaxed too. One time at playgroup, not too long after I stopped lying, one of the mothers told me what a relief it was to stop pretending. For moral reasons, but also because she always forgot she'd shoved the dirty dishes in the oven when we came, and regularly filled the house with smoke and trashed a muffin pan when she turned the thing on for dinner.

Not all of the mums were down with it. One of them said that she thought that because she was home with the kids it was her job to care for the home. (She said this while she made a slightly disgusted face, noticing that her crawling baby was collecting cat hair on a trip to the toy box in my living room.) I smiled sweetly and said that I was home because I was a parent, not a homeowner. Nobody had suggested I needed to quit my job and keep up with the laundry when we bought the place. I don't think she was sold, and that's okay. I hope dusting brings her a lot of happiness and fulfillment. I enjoyed painting pictures with my kids more.

Over the years, I've really gotten the hang of this. It used to be that when people came over, I apologized for the mess and made excuses for why I wasn't normal. I've been busy, the kids are sick, Joe's been away . . . now I look them dead in the eye and tell them the truth. "Sorry about the mess, but I just don't give a shit." This family does people before things, and we all mess up, and we all clean up, and we do have some basic standards of hygiene, but it's mostly about keeping the smell down and the floor clean enough that the cat doesn't get stuck to it. If I tried to have a life that was anything at all like the one you're telling me I'll get if only I use your products, I know that my family wouldn't be as happy—or at least I wouldn't be.

I don't need you to try to sell me things by showing me a life that no person could ever, ever achieve without sacrificing all of their happiness, knitting time, and the hours they could have spent smelling a baby's head. I don't need you telling me that normal people are never angry and that they all find deep personal satisfaction in scrubbing the toilet. I really don't need my intelligence insulted by your idea of normal. My teenager is slamming a door right now because I don't understand her life. You don't understand mine. If you want to sell me something, quit with the oversell. Quit with the lies, and, for the love of everything holy, stop trying to sell me cereal. I don't like it, and you put too much sugar in it. Show me your product. Show me you think it's useful or delicious, or safe, or cheap, or good for the cat, but stop showing me a family I can't ever have, wouldn't want, and one that looks sort of boring anyway.

Thanks,

Stephanie

P.S. If you want a customer for life, make a single commercial that features a man fulfilled by yogurt, scrubbing the kitchen, making dinner for his family, and admiring his freshly cleaned carpet. That's the "normal" I'm looking for.

Dear Sidney

I just named you that because it seemed awkward to write a letter calling you what I've been calling you for just about thirty years, which is "this guy who drove by me one time," or at least that's what I've called you in my head, because I don't talk much about what you did. Now that I've called you Sidney, I can tell it's all wrong. It doesn't sound mean enough.

Let me tell you something about who I was when we encountered each other, Sid. (Oh, Sid. That's better—more of an edge.) I was sixteen years old, and things were starting to look up. Not way up, but they were definitely better. I'd been an odd kid, and I suppose I'd really just graduated to being an odd teenager, but I was starting to accept it, and I had found a few friends who were odd too, and I was doing okay, especially if you compared the sixteen-year-old me with the absolute disaster that was me between eleven and fifteen. Preadolescence, if that's what you call it, hit me like a runaway train full of low self-esteem, and the worst part was that, even now, I think it was appropriate, at least given the fact that I live on Earth.

When I was eleven, I realized a few things. First of all, it really was true that Kelly Baxter was the only person in the whole school who was shorter than me. This meant that I was magnificently tiny but didn't have the glory of being the tiniest, and I think that would have helped. I should have asked Kelly, but the point is that I was short, and eleven was the age when other kids noticed. Eleven also turns out to be the age that you realize that when people tell you "good things come in small packages," they're trying to be comforting, and if there was nothing wrong with being short, nobody would bother to comfort you. Eleven was also the age that I got glasses, and I can tell you that the other kids noticed that too.

From there it was all downhill. It turned out that up until you're just about to become a teenager, differences between kids don't matter that much. There weren't a lot of eight-year-olds who cared that I loved to knit and had since I was four, but a thirteen-year-old prolific knitter who wears glasses? I might have just as well saved myself some time and worn a T-shirt that said, "Call me Granny. I like it." Somewhere in there I got braces, which was a serious point in the uncool department, and somewhere else in there every other girl in the school (including Kelly) got breasts—or at least the start of them. Me? When I was fourteen and a half, I went to the bank to open an account for my babysitting money, and when I got to the head of the line, the teller said, "How can I help you, son?" I was wearing a pink dress at the time.

I was a book reading, glasses- and braces-wearing short girl who looked like a moderately unattractive boy and really enjoyed knitting and making my own yogurt. To say I wasn't fitting in would have been an understatement, but I had a nice mother, and she'd told me this was absolutely temporary, and I believed her. A few years ago, over coffee, she told me that she'd not believed that at all. She'd hoped, with a maternal fervency, that I was going to get through that, but the situation had been so grim. "God," she said, sipping her coffee and staring out the window. "You were my kid, and I loved you, but you were not cute." I just about burst into tears, not because she'd said I was an ugly kid, but because it was a relief to know I hadn't been imagining it.

Turning sixteen mostly solved it. The year I was sixteen all the super weird things that I enjoyed suddenly made me quirky and interesting. Lots of people were knitting then, and lots of people liked to read, and as long as I kept my social group skewed toward the dork end of the scale, I did okay. The best part about being sixteen, though, was that something happened to my body. It grew up. I had a little growth spurt, just enough to put my height at the low end of normal and let me grow into my teeth, and I got a visit from the Breast Fairy. She brought me some extremely nice ones, and they landed in the right places, and I was still super skinny, but it turns out that if you stick some boobs on a skinny girl, she just looks built. I still knew I wasn't pretty. Adolescence had done nothing for my nose or my eyebrows, and I still had to wear thick glasses, but the braces had come off, and I was old enough to understand how the whole thing worked. I knew what a smoking hot body could do for you, how impressive boys thought breasts were, even if your face wasn't really beautiful, and I had started to believe that I might be okay looking, if you took the whole package together.

That's who I was, that day in the summer, when you drove by. I was someone who was getting used to maybe being okay, maybe being pretty enough to pass, and I'd embraced my future a little bit, and I was thinking that maybe, just maybe, it was possible that the boy I liked could like me back, and I was walking down the street with my girlfriends. There were about six of us, and I was giddy because I wasn't the sort of girl who usually traveled in a pack, but things were looking up. We walked down the street, and you drove by. Or maybe you weren't driving, maybe you were a passenger, because I didn't actually see you. The car with you in it went by, and the window was down, and there were a bunch of guys inside, and you were all rowdy, and then, as you passed, you yelled at me. You yelled, "Nice legs, shame about the face." You yelled it loud enough for all my friends to hear.

My face burned with embarrassment, my eyes welled with tears, I turned my face away from the other girls, and they turned away too. I know you were young, and I know it was stupid, and I know you were just having fun, but it's been thirty years, and I don't want to pretend to you that it didn't matter, or that it didn't make a difference. I know you intended it as an insult, but that wasn't how I took it. To me, it was confirmation. It was everything I'd known in my heart and thought I could overcome. It was like you knew that I was thinking that maybe I'd evened out a bit, and you wanted to let me know that it was pointless. My shiny new breasts and curved hips and fabulous thighs, they weren't enough to make up for the face, and I wouldn't ever be the sum of my parts, and I wasn't pretty, and I never would be. In that moment, I knew everything I'd ever need to know about my looks and, Sid, that moment changed the way I handle myself, even now.

All these years later, I can tell you what you did. That day, I decided you couldn't put lipstick on a pig, and since then, I have gone with my strengths. I work out. I still have a pretty rockin' bod, especially for a woman in middle age, though it is a little thicker than it was. I still like my breasts, although they're working class now, having helped me take care of my babies, but that only made me like them more. I am very funny, and clever, and I have a good education, and I still knit and make yogurt because, dammit, I still think those things are cool. I like myself, and I've grown up enough that I know now that I have a thousand things to compensate for my face, not just my body. I don't worry about my looks. I don't wear makeup, I don't do my eyebrows. I have hair, not a hairstyle, and I know in my heart that I am not super pretty, and that's okay, Sid. It really is.

I haven't told many people this story, and I think it's because I don't want them to know what you said. I suppose I worry that it will give them ideas, like I would tell the story, and then they'll look at me and say, "Oh, wow. You know, now that you mention it, you are sort of unattractive. I never noticed before, but now that I've thought about it, I just can't stop seeing it. Do you have time for me to describe your nose to you?" I still think about that day with you a lot. It was such a small thing, such a small moment, and I don't hate you. You were just the wrong stupid teenager at the wrong time, and you weren't even creative. "Nice Legs Shame About Her Face" is a song title from The Monks, you jerk. After years of keeping this to myself, I bet you're wondering why I would write it down now, because I'm hoping you can tell that I'm not crazy enough to think that you're going to read this, Sidney, although if you do, know that I mostly forgive you, and I hope you grew up to be a lovely man.

I'm writing this because of something that happened when I was thirty-eight. One day, a Tuesday (I remember that much), my very pretty sister was explaining to me that I could be much prettier if I made an effort. I was thinking of you, Sidney, and considering telling her why I knew that wouldn't work, and that I didn't care if I was pretty, and I was going over what had happened in my head. Me and my friends, walking down the street, and you yelling what you did at me, and something happened. After all those years, after the painful impact you've had on my life, something occurred to me. There were seven of us walking down the street. It's actually possible that you weren't yelling it at me but at one of the other girls—not that it makes it any better—but I was so insecure, so afraid of how I looked and how I felt, that I took six words tossed out of a passing car and I was so sure that they fit me that I practically tattooed them on my heart.

It doesn't change the fact that you were a jerk, Sid. You yelled that at someone, and you'll have to live with that, but it turns out that it had a lot more to do with me than with you, and I just wanted to write down my part, in case you yelled at another group of girls that summer and one of them is still thinking about it. Finally—and, Sid, this has nothing to do with you—I wanted to apologize to my sixteen-year-old self, and maybe the self I've been since then. I was awfully hard on her, and in retrospect, she was so very, very pretty.

Stephanie

Dirt and Swiss Cheese

Bill Cosby once said, "There are some people who have trouble recognizing a mess." My husband is like that, at least with literal messes. He's a sensitive, loving, wonderful man who can spot an emotional mess a mile away and usually even knows what to do about it, but a literal mess? He's got a crazy high threshold where he just can't see it. It is as if he was born with a birth defect—something like color blindness—where he literally cannot see dirt or disorder of any kind, no matter how bad it gets.

When it comes to their environment, everyone has a line. A trigger point. A place where you look around you at the dishes and the dust and the cat hair and you just can't stand it anymore, and then you clean something. Some people are moved at dust bunnies. I'm moved more around what you'd colloquially refer to as "dust bison," but Joe? He is never, ever moved. I used to think that Joe's line was just in a different place than mine—a place I don't recognize, can't approve of, or condone, but a place that still exists. Now I think he has no line. There's a place where I look around and the disorder that surrounds me starts to affect my internal order. A place where the chaos has to be set to rights before it starts making me feel chaotic on the inside, or at least a place where I know that if someone came over, I would pretend not to be home. Joe never gets there. I worry, when I travel without him, that he's at home allowing people into the house to see the way he's let it get, and that they're seeing it, and they're blaming me. Absolutely nothing triggers Joe to clean, short of personal impact. He can't recognize the mess for what it is until consequences of the situation smack him upside the head.

I have conducted experiments. If the laundry needs doing, Joe won't be able to recognize that for days or maybe weeks. The overflowing laundry basket he's stepping around every time he goes into the bedroom? Can't see it. The basket of dirty towels stationed at the top of the stairs? Joe cruises by that like it's not even there. He won't see it, and I mean that. It's not until he has to confront the reality of what's happening that he knows he has to take action. He can be cruising by a nine-foot-tall tsunami of laundry, a monstrosity with whitecaps of sports socks cresting over the top, but that won't mean anything to him until he runs out of clean underwear. Then Joe will stand there, looking at his empty drawer in shock. It's been getting emptier all week, so this shouldn't come as a surprise to him, but he'll stand there, looking at the place where he was hoping his clothes would be and say something like, "My God. I think I'm going to have to do laundry."

Joe's like that with everything. The mountain of dishes piled on the counter, reeking up the place with fruit flies trying to settle on the buffet of unscraped plates, means nothing to him. Nothing until he doesn't have a plate or a glass to use, and even then I feel like it could go either way. He could survey the situation and decide to wash the dishes, or he could turn to me and say, "Wow. We should buy more glasses."

A few years ago, I redecorated our bedroom. It got new floors and a nice paint job, and I took every single thing out of that bedroom, washed it, painted it, and redid the whole thing. When I was done, I put everything back in an orderly fashion. "This," I told Joe, "is going to be a big change. A fresh start. A chance for you to be tidy."

For years, Joe had struggled with chaos in and around his dresser. He has a tendency to create what our family calls "Joe piles." They're the detritus of his day. Whatever has collected in his pockets, whatever people have handed to him, whatever he comes to possess through his day, Joe puts in his pocket. When he comes home, he empties that pile out and leaves it somewhere in the house. Two batteries, a receipt, a note to himself, a grocery list from me—whatever's in Joe's pockets at the end of the day becomes his personal seaweed and driftwood, left behind when his daily tide comes in and goes back out again. We've talked about this, and, over the years, Joe has come to understand that he cannot leave these piles all over the house.

He was slow to understand this, if only because he sees no rea-son not to put it on the counter. It doesn't look like a mess to him, and besides, in his heart, he believes that he'll be back to sort the whole thing out in a minute, which might be true, except it's not, and if it was, I would want him to clean up the piles from the last sixteen days before this one anyway.

We've made a rule over the years that Joe's piles have to be restrained to a few places. He can do what he likes with his briefcase, and he does. Every few months his bag fills up, and then usually he abandons it somewhere in the house and starts using a new one. When I find an abandoned stash, I put a tag on it with the date and stick it in the basement. It's an imperfect filing system, but it's ours. The other place we've been restrain-ing it to is the top of his dresser, and once I redid the whole bedroom it was going to be a pile-free zone. In fact, there were to be no piles at all. Joe couldn't pile up anything at all any-where in the house, because once I painted the bedroom, we were civilized people, and civilized people don't make piles on any furniture at all.

At first, it went pretty well. There were no piles. I was proud of Joe and impressed with his commitment to our new cause, and then one day, a few months after the no-pile edict, I noticed that Joe hadn't put away his underwear. Instead, they were folded, neatly and properly, and stacked in a pile on the floor by the side of the dresser. A few days later, that's where socks were too, and after a week, I took matters into my own hands. I gathered up the unmentionables, and without mentioning it, I opened his top drawer to put them away. Instantly, I realized that Joe hadn't changed. Nothing had changed. Joe hadn't been putting his underpants in his top drawer because his top drawer was full. For weeks, Joe had been putting his piles on top of his dresser like he always had, and then, remembering the new rule, had opened the drawer and swept in the lot, wholesale. I had only busted him because the drawer was full. If we had big furniture, it could have gone on for weeks more.

Joe's top drawer was such a train wreck to me that I could hardly breathe when I saw it. Truthfully, it looked like it could be the opening from a film about a hoarder. The guy would be sitting there surrounded by ten years of stuff, with the fire department cutting the wall out of his house so he could leave, and he'd say, "It started with the drawer. . . ." I can admit that I didn't handle it really well. I asked Joe to clean it up. I told him what I thought, and I yelled about hoarders, and the phrase "This is how it begins" was definitely bandied about. I told him that he should know it's time to clean up whenever the thing he's using for "Joe piles" could no longer be used for what it is. If you can't dine at the dining room table because it's got your stuff on it, it's time to clean. If you can't cook in the kitchen, that's your tip-off. Can't sit in a chair? Can't fit a coat in a coat closet? It's time to do something, I told him, when you can't keep your underwear in your underwear drawer. The whole time I was issuing this profoundly helpful speech, Joe didn't look like I was helping him. He was looking at that drawer, and he was hearing that it needed to be cleaned up, and he really didn't see how that was going to be possible.

You could be forgiven for thinking that Joe is a pig. He definitely looks like he's messy, I can tell you that, but the truth is that Joe isn't avoiding cleaning up because he doesn't care about what's happening in that drawer. In truth, he's a little immune to the dirt, but he's also a holistic thinker. Joe doesn't look at the piles he makes or the drawer he puts them in and see a job that he could tackle. He sees the entire drawer as one job, and from there it's overwhelming and impossible. He looks at the drawer or the living room or the whatever and he sees all the flotsam and jetsam of his life free floating in there. There are worthless gum wrappers next to $20 audio resistors, and Joe can't imagine that there's ever going to be time to deal with it. To his way of thinking, you'd start, and you wouldn't be finished for days. Each item would have to be considered individually, sorted, and organized, and then once you had all of the items sorted, you'd have to figure out what to do with them. In his mind, Joe thinks the only way to do it is to sit down with that drawer and start sorting, work for nineteen hours straight through, just get it done. Get takeout, call in sick, ignore the children—it would be all consuming and a mighty and earnest effort. At the end, there he would be, the house in chaos, a thousand things left undone, but before him on the table—several piles. A pile of receipts, a pile of resistors, a pile of batteries, and a pile of Things He Wanted to Save (this category includes ticket stubs, drawings by small children, and anything of a sentimental nature).

At this point, he would have a significant problem. Everything was sorted but not supposed to go back in the drawer, because, remember now, the instruction was to clean out the drawer, though it's all impossible from here. Let's start, for just one second, with the receipts. You can't throw away receipts, can you? Or maybe you can, but only the old ones, but how old do they have to be before you throw them away? Once you work that out, you'd have to read every receipt to see if it fit in that category, and the work is just starting with the receipts. The batteries? Well, to be honest, the issue with them is the same one that wound them up in the drawer. Joe knows you can't throw batteries in the garbage. This knowledge, along with not knowing what one is supposed to do with something if it can't go in the garbage, means that items that fall into this no-man's-land have to, well, stay, and if they have to stay, and if I won't let him keep them on the kitchen counter, then the catchall of the underwear drawer is the only place they can go. Sorting this stuff only opens up the wide expanse of madness that he'll be cast into once the sorting is done.

Joe's amazing and brilliant mind can see all that when he opens that drawer and sees the pile of stuff. One look, and he knows nothing can ever be done, and that makes it easy to put a little more in it. It's an overwhelming problem. Even I can see it if I look at it his way. What I can't understand is why Joe can't see it my way. When I look at that drawer, I don't see a big job—well, I do see a big job, but my brain immediately registers that it's a big job and decides to break it into pieces. I'd never sit down with the whole drawer and try to deal with it at once. I'd decide to work on it for five minutes a day until it was done. It's just the way I think, and it turns out that it's got a name. It's the "Swiss cheese method." The Swiss cheese method says that if you have a big job to do, you can't look at it holistically, or you'll be overwhelmed, the way that Joe is. The idea is that you do what you can, one step at a time, and everything you do puts one more hole in the big slice of cheese. You see where it's going, of course. A hole here, a hole there, and pretty soon there isn't that much cheese, and the job (that's the cheese that's left—it's a metaphor) becomes easy to eat. The Swiss cheese method resonates for me, but not for Joe. He can no sooner see how that problem could be handled a little at a time than he can see how there's enough cat hair on our carpet to assemble another cat.

There are advantages to being a holistic thinker. Joe is better at seeing the big picture of our finances as well as seeing the big picture of where our kids are at. I can get bogged down in the condition of the kitchen floor the same way I can be stuck on a particular thing the kids are doing. Joe can see that a moment or a day with the kids is just one day. Just as when he looks in his drawer he can see the enormity of cleaning it up, Joe can look into his children's eyes and tell that they're just not finished yet either. He sees the whole of them, and he doesn't sweat the small stuff with them the way that I'm compelled to. In a lot of ways, this holistic gift serves him really well and might be worth the mess.

Realizing this, of course, does nothing to help with the cleaning problem, but I did get a tip from his mother. When his top drawer got too bad when he was little, she just used to get rid of it by handfuls. Once a week, she'd go into his room, open the drawer, take a chunk from the back, and pitch it into the bin. "The problem never really got solved," she admits. "But it kept it from getting out of control."

"It's the Swiss cheese method," I tell her. It's not going to help Joe, I see that now. He is who he is . . . and he hasn't noticed what I'm doing with his drawer either.

Low Self-Esteem and Other Symptoms of the Chicken Pox

As I glance through my e-mail, I note that a family gathering I really wish I could attend is scheduled on the one day of the week that I can't make it. This is news I wouldn't like on any day, but today is special. Somehow, today I can grasp the full portent of someone in my family booking a family event on the one day I can't be there. I fire back an e-mail quickly, letting them know that I'm at a job that day. I hit REPLY ALL so that the whole family knows. Shortly thereafter, e-mails start coming in saying that Saturday is the only day that other people can make it, even if it means that I can't come . . . and I take a deep breath and fire back a nice reply to all of them saying something like, "Oh well. It's okay, I'm just one person. Have fun without me," but that isn't really what I want to type. At the time, it feels very big of me to type that. It is kinder than I feel like being, and it isn't sincere. I feel like I'm being very brave and special—and that should have been a warning sign.

Two minutes later, I was blinking back tears. I realized that it isn't just this family gathering that I can't go to. It's practically all of them. I was unable to go to a family dinner just the previous week. It was my husband's birthday dinner, and I couldn't go because I was out of town working. Before that, I was away, and the whole family had dinner at my mother's, and that's what they called it too—"the whole family," even though it wasn't the whole family, was it? I wasn't there, and that means it couldn't have been the whole family, unless . . . I think back further. Remember that party? I arrived late, but it really seemed like they had been having a lot of fun without me. Actually, it seemed like they didn't really even notice I wasn't there. I knew then that they all must secretly hate me. They're glad when I can't come, and probably they all sit around when I'm not there and talk about the general feeling of relief they have when they don't have to pretend to love me. I realized that this is why my entire family has been asking me for my work schedule all these years.

Sitting there, I can't believe it's taken me this long to catch on, all those times I told myself that it wasn't personal, that the minor bumps in the road were normal things. The time when my invitation didn't arrive? I can see now it wasn't mailed, on purpose, just like the way sometimes I'm not on an e-mail chain, or the time I found out that my sister sometimes has people over in the evening and those people are not me. I realize why I'm taking it all personally. It is personal, and there's only one explanation for why they would all have come to hate me like this.

I'm horrible. I'm an insensitive, terrible person. I have been accidentally offending my family and hurting their feelings for years, and I was too obtuse to know it, and the reason that nobody has ever, ever said a word to me is because they're afraid of my wrath, and because they know that I am such a hard-hearted monstrosity that there's no point in telling me. My daughters are probably in therapy about me, or they will be soon. I bet I'm about to get the bill for it in the mail. One time, I let Megan slip in the bathtub when she was a toddler, and she had to get her lip glued shut. I'd thought that didn't matter, but now I can see that it was probably the day that the dislike they have for me started. If I were them, I wouldn't even let me hold a baby. I get out a piece of paper, and, through my tears, I start listing the disastrous elements of my devastating personality and trying to figure out what I could do to make them love me again, now that I've ruined it all. I understand that I don't deserve their love, but maybe I could earn it. This list takes most of the evening, and I fall asleep on my tear-stained pillow, clutching it in my hand. Right before I nodded off, I told Joe not to worry. I would understand if he wanted to leave me.

The next morning, I woke up with a fever, and my whole body ached, and I was so congested that I could barely breathe, and it all came together. It has taken me the better part of forty years to learn that low self-esteem and self-loathing are a symptom of viral infection for me. It's such a telltale sign that I'm writing this down to try to help me remember that if I find myself thinking for even a second that my whole family has turned against me—my whole wonderful, lovely family, who would never leave me out or not want me to come to a dinner—the flaw is not in them. There's something wrong with me, and I don't mean just the way that I can be awkward at parties.

If I find myself not just sitting on the edge of the pity pool but stripping myself bare and cannonballing whole-heartedly into the deep end, not just feeling a little sorry for myself but finally seeing clearly that no one has ever loved me for who I am and that all I do is work, and the world is now and has always been skewed in a way that means I've never had a moment's happiness, and if I think all my energy is spent ensuring the happiness of ingrates with no one to blame but myself, or if I find myself weeping seasoning tears into the soup I'm making or biting back my whimpers as I sit at my desk to write, or if, as I leave to go to the grocery store, I know without a doubt that I might as well not complain about it because my life is nothing but a wasteland of servitude and quiescence, then that means I should stay away from people with suppressed immune systems and avoid kissing babies and old people, because I am coming down with something. A long time before the first sniffle, a long time before the first sneeze, days before my temperature rises or I get a sore throat or the rash crops up, there's always something wrong with my happiness. A surging high tide of sadness, certainty that I am not loved, regret for my wasted life, they all sweep over me.

Once I figured this out, I started talking about it, and I learned that I'm not the only one with an emotional indicator for a physical illness. I've got a friend who knows he's coming down with something when he realizes that everything he's ever done in his entire life was a complete waste of time and starts to hold himself accountable for the impact that skipping math in the ninth grade has had on his career. My sister can spot an impending influenza by the way that she suddenly is able to understand that no man is going to love her and she's going to die completely alone. My friend Sue? She can tell she's getting sick because her normally lovely husband turns into a total jerk, starts picking on her constantly, and doing things deliberately to hurt her, like loading the dishwasher wrong and putting that onesie on the baby that has three snaps missing, even though she's told him she doesn't like it. Jen? Jen becomes possessed of a burning hatred for anyone she feels is narrow-minded, and her scope for whom that describes increases with viral load. By the time she's running a fever, Gandhi and Mother Teresa look provincial, intolerant, and uncharitable to her.

It's odd that there could be emotional side effects to a viral or bacterial invasion, but that really seems like what's happening. I wonder if we could use it as an early warning system. Me, I can't tell it's happening until I'm sick, and then hindsight shows me that I might have been a tad premature in thinking that I don't deserve to be in my family because I am the only one with curly hair and I don't fit in. The knowledge always seems to come too late, after the emotional tsunami has hurt me as much as the streptococcus A has. If people knew that we were like this, couldn't they help us? When Sue tells her husband that if he wants a divorce all he has to do is ask, instead of dressing the baby funny, maybe he could just take her temperature.

Science should be interested in this phenomenon. If it were studied, if it were assessed, if we could figure out how much self-loathing or insecurity were related to illnesses, with the right training and insight, this could become a diagnostic tool. There could come a day when you'd go to the doctor, and she'd ask what the trouble is, and you'd say, "Well, this morning the coffeepot broke, and that revealed to me that I have really let down my children in every meaningful way possible." Then the doctor would look at you and scribble notes and ask something like, "Have the children said so?" When you explained that, no, the children hadn't said so, but that you didn't believe them, partly because of the coffeepot, and partly because the little one looked shifty and he always looks shifty when he's lying, the doctor would consult a big book of insecurities and then announce that tomorrow you would certainly have a yeast infection.

In time, we could learn all the correlations. Fear of abandonment, and the certainty that you will die alone, far too young? Influenza. The sudden and certain knowledge that the time you spilled soup on your mother-in-law has never been forgiven, and you probably can't speak to her ever again and should probably divorce her son as a gesture of contrition? Gastroenteritis. Developing the belief, overnight, that your husband has been putting the spoons in the drawer the wrong way around not because he's clueless but because he has probably been having an affair and wants her to come into your marriage as a sister–wife because you're so inadequate that this is the only way he could ever have a real chance at happiness? If you're setting an extra place at the table for the imaginary mistress while you sob, "My God, I've been a fool," maybe you should be screened for cancer.

Who knows how it works? Maybe there's some subtle chemical that's the by-product of viral replication, or perhaps it's just that the leading edge of an illness is only subtle enough to register emotionally, but not physically just yet. I've occasionally wondered if it's some strange immune response that's a way of trying to get me to rest. I don't know what the advantage would be, considering all I do is cry there when I'm like that, but I don't understand everything about nature anyway. Just look at the platypus or the naked mole rat.

When my kids were little, I knew without being told that a kid who spent the whole day falling apart was a kid who was probably coming down with something. I'd put them to bed early, make sure they got extra-good food, a cuddle, some kindness, and understanding. Their sensitive, touchy, and upset behavior was a trigger to get me to take extra-good care of them, and I guess that's sort of useful, until you're forty and nobody tucks you into bed with a hot toddy and sympathy if you're a raging lunatic all day. They just call you crazy lady and tell you to get a freaking grip.

I've accepted that the pre-illness craziness is a normal thing for me and a normal thing for most people probably, although I think some people who are not me are better at identifying the state or beating it back. The question is really where it comes from. How come, as we start to come down with something, some of us get paranoid, some of us start seeing all the flaws in other people, and some people, such as me, only see what's wrong with ourselves? Is it that we're really a little bit like that all the time? We're always insecure or mean or anxious, and being under the weather just wears us down enough that we can't beat the feeling into submission the way we usually do? Perhaps, as our immune system fails, there's a lowering of all of our defenses—physical, emotional, and spiritual—but the weakness of the flesh reveals your weaknesses of spirit while it's at it. You have a trick self-esteem instead of a weak gallbladder or a wonky knee? It makes me wonder if this could be useful to therapists. We could go in, get injected with the chicken pox, and then wait for the virus to take hold and cut through years and years of work, getting straight to the root of our problems, revealing our most fragile selves.

I don't know how it works, or why it works, but I know it's true for me and maybe for you. I've written it down here so that the next time I'm sure that my mother-in-law is only being sweet to me so that my divorce from her son is quick and painless, I might remember what's going on and stock up on tissues.

The Physics of the Human Adolescent

Adolescence is a trying time. The entire time my kids were teens, all I worried about was getting us all out alive, more or less emotionally and spiritually intact, with a modicum of respect for civilization and without any of us doing hard time in a cell with a roommate nicknamed "The Fist." My daughters and I, we're all too pretty for prison. The amazing thing about the way adolescence goes is that while it's happening, there's not a lot of clarity. Emotions are so big during the teen years, so many new responsibilities are coming to bear, so many changes are happening—and I hear it's really hard on the teenagers too. Now that my girls are all old enough that they couldn't be charged as a minor if they committed a serious crime, I've figured out a lot. I know now that teenagers have a crappy sense of irony but a fantastic hypocrisy meter. I learned that kids who share their rooms share everything better, maybe for the rest of their lives, and that there's absolutely such a thing as a curling iron that is too hot. I've learned that when my grade ten science teacher told me I should really pay attention because the principles of physics were actually important, she wasn't totally full of it. It took twenty years to figure out how they applied, but there I was, the mother of teenagers, and I was thinking that I was glad I skipped English class instead.

There was this guy, Werner Heisenberg, and he was a physicist, and I learned about him in high school. He was the first person to assert the observer effect of quantum mechanics, which is to say that he believed that observing a system has to alter its state, and he turned out to be spot on. Werner said, "We have to remember that what we observe is not nature herself, but nature exposed to our method of questioning." In simple language, he meant that once you start trying to figure out how something works, that thing changes because of what you're doing to try and figure it out. When physicists allow for the Heisenberg uncertainty principle (it's so great that they named it after him—his mother must have loved that), they look for the influence they're having on their experiments. A great example would be an evil scientist boiling a vat of acid and trying to figure out how long it needs to boil or how hot it needs to be before it becomes a deadly vapor. If he puts the thermometer in at the moment he sees the vapor, he'll have it wrong, because (and, see, I would never have thought of this) putting in the room-temperature thermometer changed the temperature of the hot acid, just as adding an ice cube to your cup of coffee does.

The evil scientist could try putting the thermometer in when he started heating up the acid so that he would know precisely what temperature the acid had to be when it turned into a noxious death cloud, but he wouldn't know how long it took to make a death cloud. The experiment would have only revealed how long it takes to make a death cloud if you have acid with a thermometer in it. The real time could be a little different—or maybe not—but if I were an evil scientist committed to making a death cloud, I would want a lot of accuracy.

Another classic example is what happens when you try to check the pressure on a tire. When you put the gauge on, some of the air pretty much has to leak out, and therefore, in an attempt to figure out what's going on, you changed what's going on. I see it when I teach knitting classes. The minute I walk behind someone to see how they're doing, they get nervous, and then they knit like an idiot. I'd be a fool to think that this is how they really are as a knitter, but all it is possible for me to see is how they knit when they're nervous. My point, and I do have one, is that this happens with kids too. If you walk into a room full of a bunch of kids who are plotting something heinous and say, "What's up, guys?" you will instantly change their plan. At the very least, the nervous ones will rethink their involvement, since your arrival just reminded them that parents exist and are a real and persistent force, and the braver ones (realizing the same thing) are probably now shifting the plan in a more sophisticated direction. (The astute among you will note that interfering with an adolescent planning session just made some of them harder to catch and others easier. Gauge your audience carefully.)

This observer effect is vital to understanding the modus operandi of the common adolescent. Observing a teenager, as long as they know you're doing it, can discombobulate them to the point that they might fall under your control—or at least your understanding—for whole moments at a time. Done right, you don't even have to directly observe them. They just have to worry that you might. When my eldest was sixteen and went to her first party, I planned carefully. I asked where the party was, who was going, and then told her to have fun. I even dropped her off, waving good-bye at the curb. Then I went home, had a cup of coffee to kill an hour, and then drove back over, just to make sure she was having a good time and had her keys. I walked right through that party, kissed her on the cheek, said I was so glad she was having fun, and then split. The horror in the room was palpable. The parents of every kid in that room should have dropped a fruit basket off at my house as a thank-you, because, by showing up, I had successfully applied the observer effect. I'd opened the door to the idea that any parent could show up anytime and see what they were up to, and I promise you, it changed their behavior, and it changed it for a long time. Six years later, I heard Amanda warn her little sister that I was a lunatic who once came to a party, and to keep that in mind. If only they knew I wasn't crazy, I just hadn't skipped science class with any real conviction.

It turns out that teenagers are also driven by Newton's first law of motion. Newton's first law states that an object at rest will remain at rest, unless acted on by an unbalanced force, and that an object in motion continues in motion, unless acted upon by an unbalanced force. In this observation of your teen, consider the teen the object and you the force, and remember that this law of physics doesn't mean that you have to be unbalanced with your kid, although I always sort of was. The idea of an unbalanced force means that you have to be more interested in your kid doing something (or stopping something) than your kid is. Practically applied, this means that your kid will stay at rest (in bed, on the couch, in front of the computer) until acted upon by a force greater than they are—you. It also means that a kid in motion will stay in motion and on course until they're acted upon by an unbalanced force that takes them off that path. This means that if your young darling has started doing homework, they're probably going to keep doing it until they get a text from someone cuter than you. (Protip: All their peers are cuter than you.) That peer influence is an unbalanced force if I ever saw one, and that will be enough to knock them off course or cause them to come to a stop. (This is, by the way, a really great reason to limit cell phone use during homework time—or just smash it to a million pieces with a heavy hammer. Whatever feels right in the moment. You gotta trust your instincts.) There is an upside, though, because it means that if you get a kid pointed in the right direction, say, helping someone, or cleaning out the garage, or trying to solve a problem of social justice, they'll work like nothing you've ever seen before. Just don't get in their way if you can possibly help it.

There are other concepts I've found helpful, such as the causality principle, which says that every effect has a cause, and which means that a teenager can't actually say that being late "just happened" or claim that the relationship between their study habits and their grades is, in fact, "total bull crap." Similarly, they are not broke because I am refusing to give them money. They are broke because they spent all their babysitting money on lip gloss, and that's just the way the world works, rather than all the proof you need that I am a mean mother. Ours is a world of cause and effect, and that means that I can't accept that this kid doesn't know what happened to the fourteen pounds of groceries I put in the fridge this morning.

No matter what your teenager says, there is also the principle of "no creation ex nihilo," which means that something can't come into existence out of nothing. This has been used against my girls when they want to know why they're not getting pocket money, even though their rooms have just spawned three new kinds of fungus and the cat's been lost in there for three days.

It's Latin for, "Get a job and then you won't be so broke." Its counterpart, "No demise as nihil," means that something cannot become nothing, and that's a lesson about teenaged self-esteem if ever I heard one. That principle says that it doesn't matter what goes wrong, what people say, or how big your mistake or your pimple is. You're something, and you can't become nothing. You're important. You have a right to be here. Or at least in your room with the spores.

Finally, I've come to understand that Newton's third law of motion is probably the most important one of all when it comes to parenting. This law states that for every action, there is an equal and opposite reaction, which explains why your teenager flinches away from you when you try to hug them. It also explains where I'm going wrong as a parent. Any time I've tried a form of discipline and gotten behavior from a kid that made no damn sense, I've remembered this principle. Any time I say something and my kid goes right off the deep end, I remember that I probably provoked that response. I know my kid is a great kid at the heart of it, so if I get a bad reaction to my parenting, I look at what I did.

Newton's third law has pointed out some of the worst mistakes I have ever made, when I saw the equal and opposite reaction in my child. Every time I tried to control them and that push only sent them further out of my grasp, and every time I invaded their privacy only to have them create more barriers between us, and every time I said too much and got a kid who said nothing, Newton's third law is the best reason I can think of to be firm and kind and, most of all, gentle with a teenager.

After all, adolescence is a difficult phase for everyone involved, and you're both going to have to hold on to what you can. Rely on physics, hold fast to the rules that govern all, and if you have to skip anything, consider history. Science is too useful.

Losing the Room

I was working my way through the room, and everything was going the way it always does for me at parties. I am not the sort of person who is very good at parties. I am the person at parties who should really be in the kitchen, washing cups and making drinks and putting parsley on things. This was someone else's party, though, and I hadn't yet found my way into their kitchen to garnish anything, so instead I was wandering around the soiree with my usual strategy in force, which is to cling desperately to the person I came in with, as though they were a social life raft. I stand right beside them for the whole time, no matter where they go or what they do, and when there's a lull between conversations, I mutter endearing things to them, things like, "Don't leave me." My fear has always led me to believe that this is fun for both of us, but really it only leads to certain abandonment as the person I've tied myself to eventually responds to this pressure by ditching me or locking themselves in the bathroom. This evening, the abandoning shlep is my husband. He has wandered off with some other engineer and will most likely surface later in the kitchen, getting drinks and putting parsley on things, but in the meantime, I am wandering the party alone and trying to avoid talking to people. It isn't that I don't like people. I quite do, it's just that I like them in small doses or in a way that's intimate and not like this—not at all like this. This is more like being lined up in front of machine gun fire and trying to get through it, because I suck at small talk. To me, it feels like a barrage of wildly unpredictable questions, such as, "How are you?" or "Are you enjoying the summer?" I believe in my heart that this stranger really couldn't care less, so pretty soon I start worrying that they won't be very interested in my answers, or that my answers won't be very good, and then I start to get nervous, and then I start to talk, and the more I talk, the more risk I know I am taking.

I don't have many superpowers. I'm really good at making very big dinners, and I can play the melody of any song I know on just about any instrument. As you would imagine, the former is way more useful than the latter, but my biggest gift is that of charm. I know it's hard to imagine someone who's as shy and nervous at parties as I am being charming, but I have worked hard to cultivate some social graces. For someone who's socially fearful, being charming makes the world an easier place to negotiate, and it has been a powerful skill. I work hard at being likeable, I work hard at avoiding conflict, at greasing social wheels, at generally pleasing people, and this works well everywhere I go, but especially at parties, where (along with my sense of humor) it is essentially my entire defense mechanism. If this system fails, I will have nothing. The idea of being defenseless and bare in a group of people is so horrifying to me that I have been known to panic and tell random knock-knock jokes to overcome the moment.

There's a concept in stand-up comedy and any sort of public speaking called "losing the room." It happens when what you're saying or doing becomes uncomfortable for the other people in the room, and they stop being able to truck with what you're saying. They disengage, and you can feel it happen. There are a lot of ways to make people uncomfortable. You can challenge a belief, bring up a topic that's taboo, talk more than they would like, or, ironically, not as much as they would choose. You can accidentally violate a cultural expectation, or say something too intimate too soon. I, personally, specialize in bringing up a strong opinion with a particular group, only to helplessly discover, as I feel the room begin to slip away from me, that I am explaining this view to a group of people who could not possibly be more opposed to my point of view or have a better reason to feel reviled by my choices.

Allow me to illustrate. Picture me, abandoned at a party, finding myself accidentally in a knot of people who have formed around me, believing that I would not be standing by the dip if I were not really interested in a chat. We start talking, they ask me if I have any kids or pets, and I say that I have three grown girls who have mostly moved away and a cat who still lives with me. Someone asks me if I have a dog, and it happens. Instead of just saying no, I start to think that I can get out of this by being charming. I'll entertain them, I think, and they won't notice that I'm really not good at this, and so I begin explaining at great and impassioned length that I do not have a dog and back it up with the many robust and well-formed lifelong reasons I have for disliking dogs. I have, of course, forgotten the clear cultural quirk that only terrible people dislike dogs (and pie, which I also hate—never tell someone you don't like pie) and that disliking dogs instantly demonstrates to people that your heart is empty of joy and kindness, and am now listing my very valid reasons. I have begun my litany with the tendency canines have to enjoy inappropriate touching and have now moved on to the way that I hate that they don't have the willpower to save food for later. As the silence grows around me, while I expound on how I am really not into carrying around the feces of another mammal in small bags while on otherwise pleasant walks, I can feel that something has gone wrong. They're all looking at me with nothing short of violent contempt when I abruptly notice that three of the people I am talking to are wearing "I love my dog" buttons, and the guy to whom I am currently explaining that wanting a dog is like choosing to have children who never grow up is right this minute wearing a T-shirt that says, "I'd probably like you if you were a dog."

That, my friends, is "losing the room." Whatever charm and affection you may have held sway with these people earlier, that's all gone now. Unless you've got some other talent (I would suggest singing, but have seen it go 'round the drain too), your party is over. You're doomed to spend the rest of the evening walking around trying to find a place to hide while those people walk around telling other people how you hate dogs and asking other guests what sort of a person hates dogs while they glance at you like they've just recognized you as the winner from a puppy-kicking contest. Don't worry, though, they're going to leave as soon as they've told everyone, because they have to go to a dog lovers' club meeting. After all, they are the executive committee. You're left at the event with your spouse locked in the bathroom, the dip clearly off-limits, standing haplessly next to a framed picture of the host's golden retriever until you can get out. That room is lost. All you can do is shut up until it's over and never go back. You're not going to be able to fix it. You can't explain that you have met some very nice dogs that you were able to like on an individual basis, or that you're sure their dog doesn't do any of the things that you don't like about dogs, or even tell them that meeting them has changed you, and that you're going straight to the dog rescue place to get one. It's too late. You've lost the connection, and forging it again is impossible. The room is lost, and you with it.

This is what I am afraid of at parties. That my charm will fail me, and there will be nothing left, and that then the fear will overwhelm me, and my panic will guarantee the outcome. This is also what I am afraid of at speaking engagements, except there I also feel sure that somewhere in the room is a person who has, of their own free will and with great determination, bought a ticket or stood in line to see me, and they have known with complete confidence, since they decided to attend, that I am going to be terrible. They're only here to get the proof. I know they are there, and they're going to contribute to my personal disaster and the fear I feel, and once I'm nervous, I'll rely on my charm, and if my charm should fail, I'll panic—and this, by the way, this is how I came to be at your party, standing by the dip, and talking about how your grandmother was probably a hooker.

I was talking about crochet, and that afghan she made was really nice, and I'm sorry I bolted out of your front door without explaining. I'd lost the room.

Quite Pretty in Person

It's happened several times now. The first time, I totally let it go. It didn't register. I was moving fast. Then it happened again, and I started to think about it. When it happened a third time, the resonance hit me like a train.

I was teaching at a retreat—the sort of event where you arrive and are thrust into the middle of strangers, and you have a few days to get to know them, and they get to know you. This isn't my best thing. I am very shy, although I'm proud that I don't come across that way. It's taken me forty-five years to learn coping strategies for the defects of my basic introverted and quirky personality, and they include my best attempts at humor, charm, and deflection, and, at this point in my life, they are a reflexive, defensive posture. This event was a knitting retreat, and it meant that I was strapped to a life raft that I feel great about. I love knitting. It's the simple act of pulling one loop through another using a stick in ever more creative and complex ways, and although there are oceans of non-knitters who wouldn't believe it, it's absolutely gripping. I'm not the only one who feels this way, and so a knitting retreat is a perfect place for me. The other knitters and I love the same things, we find the same things interesting, and eventually this helps me to feel like I'm walking among my people, and I almost stop flinching and worrying. I'd been using knitting as a crutch to be able to interact with other people for two days until my book signing, when a very, very nice woman approached me, gently put her hand on my arm, and then confided the thing. "You know," she said, rather conspiratorially, "you're much prettier that you look in your pictures." Then, while I was still reeling, she took my picture, which was incredibly ironic, and faded into the crowd.

In those first minutes, I had thanked her. It had felt like a compliment, and if you had seen her face, you would get that it was clearly the way she intended it. I filed it under "kindness" until that night in my hotel room, where I did what any person with a slightly fragile self-esteem, a mirror, and an Internet connection would do. I looked at pictures of myself, and I obsessed over what a statement like that means.

I have no illusions about my appearance. I know I was prettier, in a standard sort of way, when I was younger, and I do not have the sort of face, or body, or even breasts that have been improved by the things I have done and experienced so far. I envy people who get the sort of lines on their face that say that they have spent the majority of their time smiling, but that's not the way mine have landed. My wrinkles and creases have fallen in a place that says that for the majority of my life, I've been concerned. I guess that's fair. I do worry a lot, and think a lot, and I am concerned about lots of things, from what spiders might be planning, to my children's happiness, to trying to do the right thing about recycling. These lines are here not because I haven't been laughing but because I was listening to people carefully before I laughed. I suppose there are worse things, but it isn't what I think when I honestly look at myself. What I think is that I have these worry lines and strange hair. It's curly and unpredictable, and I'm enchanted by the idea of a "hairstyle," where someone gets the same result when they do the same thing to their hair every day, but that's just not how mine works. Rather, it turns out that my hair seems to enjoy the element of surprise. I am in the latter half of my forties, quite short, and slightly dumpy, and I know that "willowy" is a word that could only be applied to me if I were stapled to that sort of tree. I have a nose that was upturned in a cute fashion when I was a kid but now looks more like a ski jump. I wear fairly thick glasses and I am petite (that's polite for short) but shouldered like a diminutive linebacker, and my legs are functionally stumpy and strong, rather than long and enticing. I have high cheekbones, now rather sadly balanced by what my family album tells me will eventually, absolutely become jowls, and I have my grandfather's thick and robust eyebrows. I am not, I can honestly say, a pretty woman.

That was what I was thinking as I looked at myself and at the pictures that came up when I searched. I've written several books, and it's not at all uncommon for someone to want a picture of us together, a record of the moment that we shared when we met, so I can quickly find a raft of them on the Internet. While pictures are records of a moment, they aren't, I realize, the moment itself. I've taken thousands of pictures and been overwhelmed at how inadequate they can be at capturing the moment that was happening. I have a framed picture of my daughter Sam, about a year and a half old, and she's lying on the kitchen floor, bathed in sunlight, watching a ladybug track a path in front of her. I love that picture. It's one of my favorites, not because of what you can see, but because of what you can't, which is that two minutes after I snapped it, Sam reached two chubby, precise baby fingers out, picked up the little bug, and popped it in her mouth. She ate it while we all watched with horror, and every time I see the picture I feel what I felt when it happened. You would see a sweet baby enchanted by a wee bug, but I see Sam with black and red wings in her teeth. This, I realize, might be part of what the lady meant, but in reverse.

The truth is, I thought, as I examined my nose and hair and shoulders in the cadre of pictures spread across my laptop screen, that cameras capture what is actually happening, what you actually look like—with a small plus or minus for the skill of the photographer, the kindness of the lighting, and whether or not you're particularly photogenic. Pictures record you without judgment, without prejudice, and without anyone there to explain that although you look mean in the picture you were really just listening, or that you were talking at the time, or that your mouth looks funny. I can come across badly in a picture, but the truth is that, as upsetting as it is to see a picture of myself where I look like I'm crazier than a bag of wet weasels, I can't explain it away. I have to accept that sometimes I look like a lunatic. It had to have been happening or it couldn't have been recorded. I look at another picture, one in which I am inexplicably flaring my nostrils and pointing at the ground, and I realize something terrible. That lady is wrong. I am not prettier than I look in those pictures. I look exactly like that. Precisely like that. Those are my nostrils, apparently I flare them, and the question isn't why I look like that. It's why she thinks I'm prettier than that at all.

Several weeks ago, I traveled to visit my uncle. He had become very, very ill, very, very quickly, and to try and prepare me, my mum had described him and warned me several times about how different he looked. How thin, how frail, how very much unlike himself. I went into his house full of trepidation, and when I saw him, I was shocked. He was a shadow of the man I'd known, rapidly eaten up by the cancer inside him that was clearly stealing his life. For two beats of my heart, I was breathless, and then a miracle happened. He spoke, and the man I had known my whole life asserted itself. The strong hands I've held since my childhood appeared like an overlay, his voice filled out his face, his smile added pounds to his frame, and within moments, I couldn't see what the disease had done. I saw my uncle. He was handsome, strong, funny, and proud, and he looked that way to me for the rest of the visit. The love and experience I had of him colored his appearance in a wonderful way. He had only been that sick for a few months. It was not enough to wash away the forty-five years I'd soaked up the look of him.

Fairy lore tells us that they have a particular brand of magic, the glamour. Fairy glamours are the power of illusion, of making one thing look like another, of making something ordinary appear extraordinary, more beautiful, more charming, more compelling than it is. This, I decide, explains the relationship between people and photographs perfectly. I have long known that my husband is incapable of seeing me clearly. He's the worst person in the world to ask about my hair or my pants. By virtue of our love, he is not a guy who can see me straight. There's too much between us. It's not just his hopes for a day free of conflict that lead him to tell me that I look amazing when I know I don't, and it's not his fond hope that flattery will land him an evening of another kind of magic. It's that he loves me, and that means that, no matter how I look, our years of fondness, happiness, and the occasionally romantic escapade are imposed on what he sees. He looks at me while I scrub the toilet, and he sees a bride, a mother holding his daughters, an afternoon at the beach, the day that I repainted the living room, and all the times I helped him carry gear to the truck. He can't unsee those things, and they make me beautiful to him, even while I age and crone. It's like the way that I can't unsee the things he's done for me over the years. He could become old, fat, bald, and grizzled, and for me it will always be overlaid with the way that he was with our children—tender, sweet, young, and handsome. I love him, and so he is the sum of my entire experience of him. I will be ninety years old, and this man still won't be able to tell whether I look good in a dress, because he saw me in one when I was younger. If I really need to know if a dress flatters me, I'm going to need someone who doesn't love me. Or a camera.

I thought of all of that while I looked at the pictures of myself and thought about what that lady had said, and I think I know why it felt like a compliment. I see how I look. I know how it works. Pictures are an exact representation of how I look, but they don't allow for the glamours. This lady was saying that after meeting me, after spending real time with me and getting to know me, I have qualities that made me prettier to her. It doesn't change the way I actually look, but I think she was saying she likes me, that knowing me now, she decided I'm way better looking than I actually am. It felt like a compliment because it is. She saw something pretty on my inside and said that the layer looks good on me.

It doesn't help me feel better about my hair, and I might make more of an effort when I see a camera, but I can accept the compliment. Apparently, with a few days' exposure to my humor and my charms, I'm prettier than I look.

The Amazing Thing About the Way It Goes

The mother in the grocery store is young, pretty, and not completely unraveled, but she's getting there. She is trying to get the hell out of there—I can see that as plainly as I can see anything. She is more desperate to get out of that store than I was to grow breasts when I was sixteen and they hadn't turned up yet, and that's saying something. She is trying to buy things, things that must be mission critical, because I cannot imagine trying to go to the store with three kids in the condition hers are in for any other reason than an absolute emergency. She must be out of toilet paper or Goldfish crackers or something else that she simply can't go on without. She's jostling a baby, held in a sling on her hip, and she's got one hand up against the back of the bairn's skull, trying to keep it from getting whacked by the shopping cart as she bends back and forth to manage everything else, and this has effectively handicapped her—she's doing everything almost one-armed, although she has a surprising amount of dexterity with her elbow. Her blouse is undone, her breast mostly exposed as she tries to nurse the baby who's grumbling in a way that tells you he's not far away from an explosion that's going to make Hiroshima look like a minor event. This mother is also juggling a kid of about three, and this kid has got a lot going on. He (or she—it's hard to tell when a kid's moving that fast) is grabbing things and pushing the button that moves the grocery belt along (both theirs and the buttons of neighboring shoppers) and is singing a litany of complaints about his situation as loudly as possible, all while intermittently trying to unzip his mother's jeans, to what end I cannot imagine and refuse to speculate on. (Three-year-olds are magical creatures, like dragons or unicorns. You're never going to understand all their motivations.) There's another kid, of about five years old, I'd guess, and judging from her body language, she's quite intent on being pissed off. I have sympathy for her. I'd be pissed off too if I had demanded my mother buy me a million things a million times and had still been refused. Her arms are crossed tightly over her chest, and she's saying things like, "But why can't we buy red candy?" while the crocodile tears well up and she stamps her feet. The kid's clearly weaponizing her emotions, and any minute now she's going to take it out on the whole world. The mother's eyes are a little wild, but she's mumbling soothing things I can't really make out, though I know that it's something like, "There, there, we'll have something so nice when we get home." I think she's mostly talking to herself, and if I were her, the something nice I'd be getting when I got home would be gin.

I'm watching, and I'm amazed. A normal person, any normal person, would be crying by now. I have raised three children, I've been her, and I can't imagine not being reduced to hitching, sloppy sobs by her circumstances, but I know that when it was me, I wasn't any different. She's trying to put groceries on the belt while someone else takes them off, and that person is also trying to render her naked from the waist down, all while she's partly naked from the waist up and another tiny but powerful mortal tries to literally suck the life out of her, while a third party (who would be considered a terrorist in some circles) demands that she comply with her desires while threatening public humiliation, pain, and unending rage. Any person, being completely abused in this manner all while attempting to do nothing more than procure the things that she needs to care for her family with her own money, should be crying by now. Slaves are treated better than this, but the mother is kindly putting down the candy revolt, checking her pants, patting the baby, and loading a cart, all with nothing but a slightly desperate look on her face.

The lady in line behind us, though, is rolling her eyes and sighing heavily. She's annoyed that the mother and her children are slowing up her progress and is having no trouble letting the world know that this is harder on her than it is on the mother or the kids. Despite the fact that all humans start as babies and go on to become children, long before they're judgmental, harsh people in a hurry, the lady behind me is shifting her weight from foot to foot, acting like babies have nothing to do with her and have no right to be in the grocery store—and certainly no right to nurse there. I feel like pointing out that she's totally unfair. That mother is legally obligated to provide those kids with food, which covers both the shopping and the nursing. This woman is oozing nasty contempt, and I can tell that she's itching to say something.

I know that if I reminded her that she was once a three-year-old ripping up a grocery store her immediate reaction would be an appalled "I was not," as though she skipped right over her own childhood and arrived here fully formed. If you dared to imply that she could have a child of her own act this way, there would be visible curls of outrage coming out of her nose. Never, ever was she a dirty, obnoxious sound machine, getting in the way of important adults doing important things (and we will pause here to point out that both of the women are doing the same important thing, grocery shopping), and I can tell that she's sure that if she were that mother, she would have a grip. Her children would be quiet and tidy and proper, and she wouldn't let them nurse in public, she'd have them trained to be hungry only where and when they were allowed to be, and when she asked them to sit quietly, they would, no matter the time of day. This lady thinks she would have children who would be doing chores, learning their times tables, and wiping things, and never raising their voices in adult company or trying to dry their nose on her skirt while spitting an apricot pit into her hand, and she'd certainly never be the sort of mother who then put the pit in her pocket and forgot about it until later when she had to hand her mate the car keys and he got the slimy thing instead.

When people like this woman are hard on mothers and fathers (but mostly mothers, because we still live in a world where mothers aren't doing a good enough job and people are impressed if a father spends an hour at parenting), I feel like I should stand on a soapbox and make a speech. I've practiced it a thousand times, and the introduction would outline several tenets of the Geneva Convention—the international collection of laws that govern the humanitarian treatment of people engaged in war. I want to tell them that the mother standing there with banana in her hair and a screaming three-year-old attached to her right thigh while being treated more poorly than a war criminal deserves your respect. Think about this. I want to say: The Geneva Convention maintains that no person should be subject to outrages upon personal dignity, in particular humiliating and degrading treatment, and you're looking here at a woman who has absolutely been urinated or defecated on in the last week and is in a bizarre arrangement where she's not supposed to even mind. Prisons have been shut down for that, and the guards court-martialed for the offense. Those children are using several forms of torture on her—things that are so cruel that they're banned in most right-minded places. Those kids are waking her several times a night for purposes she can't predict and for periods of time that vary from five seconds to four hours, and to heap insult on injury, once every month or two they sleep through the night, but just once, only enough to let hope well up in her heart before they crush it again. These people demand that she makes them food, then refuse to eat it, all while making sure that she eats cold leftovers off their dirty plates while standing up over the sink. They scream at her, and even occasionally hit her, pull her hair, and put their fingers in her nose. I can tell by the look of that three-year-old that he has tortured her by calling her name over and over and over again, even though she always answers him. Further, that baby is breastfed, and he looks like a biter. This mother is being mistreated, I want to say, and she's still planning on reading them *If You Give a Moose a Muffin* for the 835th time and helping the petulant big one sound out the words. This speech concludes with my sentiment that babies and kids are so hard on parents that I have often wondered why "child abuse" always refers to what bad parents do to children rather than what ordinary babies do to us.

I don't give the speech though. I tried out a version of it a few years ago and the response wasn't what I hoped (if by that you understand that security was involved). I keep my mouth shut, but I was overwhelmed with the urge to go up and hug that mother or catch her in some sort of embrace that means more than a hug, maybe hold her for a little while and stroke her hair and say, "I know what you're going through, and in the name of everything holy, let me carry your toilet paper to the car while you put away your right breast." I didn't do that either, because I don't want to break the spell the mother is under. That mother is doing everything amazing, under the kind of pressure that international law forbids, but she has no idea. Parenthood is like hiking from the top of one mountain to the peak of another, except it can take years to be able to look back and see how high you were before. The ability to look past it, to not see what's happening while you're doing it, is an essential self-preservation skill. You can't know what's really going on, or not only would it be impossible, but you'd spend all your time weeping softly into a mug of tea, and we're only talking about regular parenting here. My kids were totally ordinary, and they have still done things to me that, had they been any other person in my life, I would have divorced them or had them arrested, but instead I just made another dinner and read four books about toilet training. Parenthood is all about the moment. You can't look ahead or behind or you'd just be too shattered by the responsibility and fear—for yourself and for the kid. It is all just what you're doing right then, and one of the most comforting things about it is that you don't need to problem solve too much. It's an endurance game. Anything crappy your kid is doing, they'll probably grow out of. We're really just reading parenting books to kill time while the kid gets old enough to quit putting things up their nose or starts sleeping at night. It doesn't need fixing, it just needs time. It might be replaced by something else, but at least you're on to a different thing.

The amazing thing about the way it goes is that it does go. While you are in it, you have no sense of time passing, at least not properly. I remember those being some of the longest days of my life, and then looking up and trying to figure out how all those kids had got so tall in a heartbeat and being sad that it was ending. That mother just thinks it's Tuesday, not one of the most incredibly demanding days of her life, and she has no idea that she's amazing. All around us, people are doing this, starting with a person who weighs less than a turkey and then doing whatever it takes to turn them into a completely unique human being. Einstein did this to his mother, and so did Plato and Gandhi, and I bet Nelson Mandela put his mother through a hell of a time, and their parents had no idea what they were making. None of us do; we just know it's illegal not to keep trying.

I have seen parents endure amazing things. Regular parenting is hard enough, but some parents are asked to step up and endure pain that is unreasonable, pain that breaks their hearts over and over and over again, and there they are. They just do it, and that's the risk every one of us takes when we decide to become a parent. Every adult in prison, every homeless addict you see on the street, they all have a mother, and I bet most of their mothers made their way through days like this, and I promise you two things. How their mothers handled their meltdown in a grocery store probably has less to do with where they've ended up than most of us good parents hope, and they probably still love their kid, as hard or as easy as it might be to do so. Not every kid grows up to be someone who's easy to explain at a party, and despite that difficulty, not many mothers end up totally resigning the job—although, remembering what it was like, I can't believe the news isn't full of stories of parents who claim to have lost all their kids on camping trips.

I want to tell all that to the woman in line behind us in the grocery store, the woman who's impatient with the mother, and I want to remind her that she's in the presence of greatness. This mother is doing the hardest thing, and there are a thousand hard things ahead of her. Her heart is going to be broken, she's four years away from a good night's sleep, and she's making a thousand sacrifices a day, and through the miracle of love, she hasn't even really noticed. She's protected by some kind of stunning field that keeps her living in the moment, reading one more story, making one more meal, and enduring one more judgmental woman in the grocery store. I smile at that mother as she does her level best to make some nice people for us to share our planet with, and I try to look supportive. I won't give a speech, I won't burst the protective bubble she's in. I'll just try to telegraph to her, as she attempts to keep these small humans alive, that I think that she's nothing short of extraordinary, miraculous, brave greatness, and that I think it's great that there's banana in her hair.